THE COMPLETE GUIDE TO BUILDING GOOD CREDIT

AN EASY-TO-FOLLOW PLAN TO TAKE YOU FROM BAD
CREDIT TO ROCK-SOLID CREDIT IN LESS THAN
A YEAR

JENNIFER HOLLINGSWORTH

CONTENTS

INTRODUCTION

When handling your finances, keeping your credit profile healthy is important. Your credit score affects many things in life, from getting approved for loans to renting an apartment and sometimes finding a job. The credit system may be confusing and out of reach. It's easy to feel overwhelmed and not know where to start. This book breaks down everything about credit in a simple, easy-to-follow way.

This book does not focus on boring business jargon or long-winded stories. What you'll find here is an easy step-by-step guide to understanding your credit score. The book will guide you through the ins and outs of credit reports and scores. You'll get real techniques to improve your credit score in less than a year.

Each chapter focuses on aspects of building credit, such as reviewing your reports, disputing errors, and creating a repayment plan. You'll also get helpful tutorials for things that always leave you scratching your head, like navigating confusing credit bureau websites.

Besides presenting facts on improving your credit, this book is a long-term resource. Whether you're learning about credit or working on fixing bad credit, you can always refer back to this book. The strategies here will serve you for years as your credit situation changes. With practice, getting a strong score is doable for anyone. A higher score means lower loan rates and more financial freedom.

Maybe bad credit has held you back from big life goals like homeownership or starting a business. Maybe there was confusion about factors or tools available for external issues like identity theft that hurt your score. However, it doesn't have to stay that way once you understand the scoring system better. This book will walk with you step-by-step.

If you're just getting started, fixing negatives, or optimizing a currently great score - you'll find value here. Think of this book as your credit coach. When big financial decisions come up, it's there as a handy reference. Besides explaining reports and planning, the book will keep you motivated to see real long-term progress.

Consistent effort is important, but achieving stronger credit is within reach.

The book will start by explaining what goes into your three-digit credit score. It'll guide you through getting your reports to check for errors. Also, you'll learn about foolproof methods to dispute mistakes. From that foundation, set goals, track spending, and reduce debt through productive strategies.

You'll soon learn to boost your profile through positive accounts and maintain healthy habits long-term. Before long, higher scores mean big savings from reduced borrowing costs. The skills you'll gain from this book to manage your finances are the most valuable outcome.

This book aims to demystify credit. By walking you through well-researched information and proven techniques, it will empower you to take control of your path toward financial freedom. Hopefully, it will motivate you to achieve your dreams through optimized credit in less than a year. Are you ready to embark on this invaluable journey to an improved credit score? Let's get started!

1

UNDERSTANDING CREDIT SCORES

In this chapter, you'll learn what a credit score is and why it's good to keep yours looking healthy. This book will break down what goes into calculating your three-digit credit score, such as payment history and how much you owe. The book will also look at the different score ranges from good to bad.

You'll also learn the areas your credit score can impact, such as loan rates, rent, insurance costs, and job opportunities. By the end of this chapter, you'll understand the basics of credit scoring and how knowing more can help you make smarter financial choices to boost your score and avoid common mistakes that can damage it.

UNDERSTANDING YOUR CREDIT SCORE

What is a credit score, and why should you care about it? A credit score, like a report card for the past handling of money, has three numbers between 300 and 850 that indicate to lenders whether you are worthy of a loan based on the information in your credit reports.

If you have loans, credit cards, and cell phone bills, they will appear on your credit reports. However, this may change if you still owe them money. The reports also include records such as how much credit you have used relative to the available limit, if your monthly payments are timely, and the duration that your accounts have been open. All this data is collected by three main credit bureaus: Equifax, Experian, and TransUnion, which then share it with lenders via your credit score. That way, the lender can find out if you are diligent in paying back borrowed money.

With high scores falling within the 740-850 band, lenders know that borrowers are less likely to default on their obligations. Thus, they issue loans or give out credit cards at reduced interest rates. Lower interest can save you a lot of money. Anything below 630 means more interest because it signals a higher risk of defaults. Your loan application may be turned down if you have a very low credit score.

Besides loans, your credit score also comes up when getting a cell phone, renting an apartment, or even applying for certain jobs. A good score proves you're reliable. But a low score makes them think you might skip out on bills, so they'll charge extra fees or turn you down.

Your score depends on five things in your credit reports:

- **Payment history (35% of score):** Lenders care most about you always paying on time. One late payment can hurt your number.
- **Credit usage (30%):** Using less available credit is better. Try keeping balances below 30% of your limits.
- **Length of credit history (15%):** Longer is better. It shows consistency over many years.
- **Credit mix (10%):** Having a few different types of accounts makes it look more solid.
- **New applications (10%):** Too many requests for new credit can delay your score temporarily.

The key is paying bills by their due date each month, even if it's the minimum. Your lenders report on-time payments to the bureaus, helping your score increase over the long haul. Taking good care of your credit opens doors by saving money on loans and keeping options available down the road. It's always smart to watch your score.

CALCULATION OF A CREDIT SCORE

Now that you know a solid credit score opens doors, it'll help to know what goes into calculating the all-important three-digit number. Different credit bureaus like Equifax and TransUnion use similar factors, weighing each a little differently in their secret formulas. Knowing the basics empowers you to maximize scoring areas within your control.

Payment History

Lenders care most about one thing - will you pay them back reliably? This factor alone accounts for around 35% of your FICO score used by most lenders. It looks at whether accounts like credit cards and loans are paid on time or have late payments. Going 30 days or more past due on one payment each year can lower your rating substantially until the late mark "ages" off your report in 7 years. Aim to autopay when possible so forgetfulness doesn't cost you points.

Amounts Owed

The amount of revolving and installment debt you carry compared to your credit limits impacts about 30% of scores. Keeping balances low on active credit cards and other accounts shows restraint. Preferably, use no more than 30% of allotted credit limits to maximize points in this scoring bucket. Steadily paying debt shrinks this ratio for gains.

Length of Credit History

Around 15% of your FICO score depends on the length of your credit history. Having a solid mix of longer open accounts in good standing benefits this area, so don't close old cards if you can help it. Newbies may bootstrap history by first becoming an authorized user on a parent's long-active card. One year of consistent on-time payments establishes an initial track record for beginning to build.

Credit Mix and New Credit

The types of credit accounts you hold, including installment loans and revolving credit like credit cards, comprise 10-15% here. A balanced mix across loan and card types serves you well. However, frequently opening new accounts in a short timeframe is also a red flag and can temporarily affect scores. Spacing new credit applications 6-12 months apart avoids this scoring pit.

Credit Inquiries

Each hard inquiry, like when you apply for new credit, affects your ratings a small amount. Too many requests over a short span are viewed as a risk sign that you're in over your head. However, rate shopping for a mortgage or auto loan within a focused period has a mitigated effect. Keep routine inquiries to a minimum when optimized credit is the goal.

Additional factors like employment history, income level, and geographic location also provide scorecard context but are outside the scope of basic rating comprehension.

HOW A CREDIT SCORE CAN IMPACT VARIOUS ASPECTS OF LIFE

Your credit score affects more than borrowing money. It affects your finances and daily life. Here is why establishing a high score should be a priority:

Your Credit Score and Interest Rates

When taking a loan, your credit score is one thing lenders look at very closely. A higher score will qualify you for better interest rates, saving you big bucks during the loan term. For a 25,000 car loan, the difference between a good rate of 3% and a high rate of 10% is over 3,000 in total interest paid. That's enough for a nice vacation! Your score also affects rates for things like mortgage loans, student loans, and credit cards. Keeping it in the excellent range means more cash in your pocket.

Rental Home Approvals

Many apartment complexes and landlords check credit as part of approving rental applications. They want to reduce the risk of renting to somebody who may have a hard time paying on time each month. A score below 620 could result in a denial. Even if approved, you may have to put down a bigger deposit or get a co-signer. Since you need a roof over your head, credit is an important part of the rental process today.

Buying Homeowner's or Renters Insurance

The cost of your insurance policy can also differ substantially based on your credit history. Insurers see payment history as a sign of fiscal responsibility, so better scores mean lower premiums. For a basic homeowner's policy, the difference between "good" and "poor" credit could be over $100 a year. When you add up renters insurance and auto policies, good credit saves a bundle on coverage costs in the long term.

Securing Credit Cards and Other Credit Products

Try applying for a new credit card or retail store credit line with bad credit - it's tough! Issuers want to feel reasonably sure you'll repay debts as agreed. A bare-bones, unsecured card may have sky-high interest if approved at all. With better credit in the mid-600s or higher, you open doors to low-rate cards, store cards, auto financing, and other credit privileges at competitive terms. Soon, extra purchasing power comes your way, too.

Job Opportunities and Background Checks

While it's illegal to deny employment solely due to credit, some employers check reports, especially for jobs handling money. Bad credit or bankruptcy could count against you then. Build a positive credit history to open appropriate career paths.

HOW UNDERSTANDING CREDIT SCORES HELPS IN MAKING INFORMED DECISIONS

Dealing with money can be complicated sometimes. A lot is going on behind the scenes that impact options for making important decisions like loans, renting a place to live, or utility deposits. Figuring out where you stand isn't always easy.

However, having all the key information at your fingertips makes navigating the twists and turns smoother. When you know what details companies look at and how different choices can play out, it's easier to pick the paths that lead somewhere good. Otherwise, it's challenging to tell what roadblocks lay ahead.

One important set of information relates to how reliably you've handled credit in the past. Lenders and landlords look at details of your credit history to assess how likely you are to repay debts or meet obligations on time each month. Even things like applying for new credit cards or loans are noted somewhere in your records for many years.

While the specifics of your credit details may not mean much yet, learning how they all fit together can change the decisions you feel confident making now and later. Several stumbles are easily avoided once you realize the "what" and "why" behind them. Other opportunities become clearer with a full picture in mind.

Understanding the Big Picture

Instead of focusing right away on specific numbers and details in a credit report, it's best to start with the bigger concept. Try placing yourself in the lender's shoes for a moment. How would you size up someone asking to borrow money from you?

One thing that would catch your eye is a pattern of taking on too much debt month after month without fully paying it down. Seeing the same account balances growing is a caution sign. It suggests this person may struggle to afford all their obligations each billing cycle. As a lender, that would make you wary about taking on more risk.

You'd also stare at late or missed payments with raised eyebrows. After all, the whole idea of lending is that the money will come back to you on the agreed-upon schedule. Late fees are no fun for anyone. Multiple dings like this on a loan or credit card payment history hint that unforeseen expenses may interfere with on-time repayment more often than not. Again, it's a valid reason to hesitate before handing over a large sum.

It can be illuminating to put yourself in the lender's shoes. Think about what might worry you if you were the one handing out money. Try picturing times when life took an unexpected turn. Maybe you lost your job, or healthcare costs piled up higher than planned. Now imagine scrutinizing loan applications in that frame of mind. You would be consistently late, or missed payments would make you pause, and seeing debts grow month after month without a dent probably wouldn't inspire much confidence either.

Lenders need to feel secure that they'll get their money back on time as agreed. Otherwise, it isn't a smart gamble from their end. If too many red flags are waving, they have no choice but to pass on taking the risk.

Building a Solid Foundation

On the flip side, continuously meeting your obligations shows excellent dependability. Keeping credit cards paid up without fail speaks volumes of your commitment to follow through. Lenders pay close attention to these demonstrations of reliability over many months or years.

Opening an occasional new credit line every so often won't necessarily cause worry either, so long as it's spaced out sensibly. As long as total debts carried from one statement to the next remain reasonable overall, a few carefully managed accounts signal no red flags. It's all about moderation and proportionality in your spending versus earnings.

If you had known these basics beforehand, chances are mistakes could have been avoided. However, it's never too late to gain clarity on the past and make informed choices ahead! By understanding potential pitfalls lurking on the financial road, you find the strength to steer clear of trouble spots through good strategies.

Whether it's saving up appropriately for a new home or car or qualifying for lower interest rates that shave thousands off a loan, the benefits compound. Your activities now directly affect options down the line when life takes new turns.

KEY TAKEAWAYS

- Your credit score shows how reliable you've been with money. The higher your score, the better deals you'll get.
- The most important is always paying bills on time. Do this consistently, and you'll have a great payment history.
- If managed well, different kinds of accounts, like credit cards and loans, affect your score. Mix it up, but pay all of it on time.
- Lenders and landlords check your score when you ask for money or housing. High scores qualify you for better offers.
- Review your report yearly to fix mistakes. Take

care of problems right away to keep your score accurate.

Turn the page to learn how to check your reports and scores, spot mistakes, and get a clear picture of your current situation. Knowing your current situation is the first step towards improving your financial future.

2

ASSESSING YOUR CURRENT CREDIT SITUATION

U nderstanding where you stand with your credit is the first step toward building a solid financial future. In this chapter, you'll learn how to get a copy of your credit report from major credit bureaus like Experian, Equifax, and TransUnion. Take a close look through the report to check for mistakes in your personal information or outdated accounts that may be dragging your credit down.

Identifying errors is important since it gives you a chance to dispute inaccurate marks. You'll also see what accounts make up your credit mix and your current score. With this full picture in hand, you'll then be able to spot areas that need improvement. The chapter will also cover the different kinds of credit inquiries and why it's helpful to know which ones could beneficially or adversely impact your goals going forward.

HOW TO OBTAIN A CREDIT REPORT AND SCORE

Building good credit means understanding where you currently stand. This begins with obtaining your credit report and score. Your credit report contains information collected about your borrowing history, such as accounts and loans you have applied for and managed. It is compiled by three major credit reporting agencies: Experian, Equifax, and TransUnion.

Experian

Experian is one of the largest credit reporting agencies. They track payment information on loans, credit cards, mortgages, and other accounts. Experian maintains a file for nearly every adult in the United States and provides consumer credit reports used by lenders to make decisions. You are entitled to request a free copy of your Experian credit report every twelve months to review the accuracy of the information in your file.

Equifax

Equifax also tracks payment history on various credit accounts and maintains consumer files in a way similar to Experian. It collects data provided to it by furnishers such as banks, retail stores, and other organizations that issue credit. Like Experian, Equifax is required by law to provide you with one free copy of your credit report each year. It is important to check both Experian and Equifax reports for completeness and accuracy.

TransUnion

The third major credit reporting agency is TransUnion. It gathers and retains details on loans, credit cards, and bills from businesses that extend consumer credit. TransUnion builds individual credit reports based on this payment information received from creditors. Like with Experian and Equifax, individuals are entitled under law to obtain one free annual copy of their TransUnion credit report for personal review.

Obtaining Reports from Each Agency

To receive free annual copies of your Experian, Equifax, and TransUnion reports, you can visit the website AnnualCreditReport. This is the only authorized source approved by the agencies to provide this service. At this site, you will enter personal identifying information to verify your identity. Then, you can choose to pull reports from the three agencies at once or on separate requests once every 12 months.

Within two to three weeks, your reports will be mailed directly to you. It is important to review each one thoroughly for accuracy. Check that all accounts and identifiable information like past addresses and employment are correct. Contact the reporting agency immediately if errors are noticed so they can be investigated and corrected to ensure the data's accuracy in your files.

Obtaining Your Credit Score

Along with reviewing your detailed credit reports, you may wish to check your credit score. This three-digit number, which ranges from 300 to 850, provides a numerical summary of your overall credit risk based on the data in your reports.

While you are entitled to one free annual copy of your actual credit reports, scores themselves have a fee. However, personal finance websites offer access to educational credit scores at no cost. For example, websites like Credit Karma provide VantageScore 3.0 credit scores from TransUnion and Equifax on an ongoing basis for free as an educational tool to help consumers monitor changes.

Regularly obtaining your free annual reports and periodically checking accessible scores can help you gain visibility into your credit standing. With awareness of current information and errors comes the ability to make improvements to build a positive credit history. This level of understanding is important as the first step to effectively managing personal finances.

HOW TO ANALYZE A CREDIT REPORT TO IDENTIFY ERRORS

Giving your credit report a thorough review may not be fun, but it beats problems catching you by surprise later. A few extra minutes to go through it spares headaches. Here is how to analyze your credit report:

Personal Information

Verifying personal information is an essential step when reviewing your report. Confirm that all identifying information is accurate.

Start with your full legal name. Read it out carefully, making certain it matches what is listed on important documentation like your driving license. A single-character mistake could potentially lead to issues.

Your date of birth is another important element to triple-check. Creditors use this to distinguish you from others who may have similar names. A single number recorded incorrectly could attach the wrong accounts to your file.

Be sure to compare your current home address in full. Also, take the time to review past addresses listed to ensure non-current entries are removed. Having outdated information could negatively impact your file.

Other identifiers, like your Social Security number and phone number, are less prone to errors over long periods than name and address details. However, it's still worthwhile to confirm that they match what you have on record.

Past Accounts

The next section shows your past loans, credit cards, and other lines of credit you've had over the years. Check them carefully.

Most accounts will fall off your report naturally once 7-10 years have passed since closing. However, every once in a while, an old account may refuse to budge after its expiration. Keep an eye out for expired entries hanging around.

Pay close attention to old loans or credit cards you settled and closed long ago. Such accounts take up valuable space that could be used to highlight your new open accounts instead.

Also, double-check details like last payment dates and account balances on loans and cards you closed recently. Minor errors could lead to a misunderstanding.

Belongings

While scrolling through, don't skimp on inspecting the "Belongings" part of your report now. Completely foreign accounts sneaking in there is more normal than you'd think, too.

Identity theft is a major problem these days. So always look for full accounts, especially the ones with late payments or collections attached, that you know you never opened yourself.

These mix-ups could have serious damage if not caught and removed. Do not deal with someone else's financial mistakes showing as your own.

Marks like late bill payments, things in collections, defaults, and bankruptcies should not damage your name without cause. Scrutinize every line with an eagle eye for anything strange or unfamiliar.

One wrong entry can cost you financing or renting opportunities if not caught early. Peace of mind is worth the preventative effort.

Discrepancies

Finally, scan the details of each tradeline very carefully. Dates, balances, credit limits—everything needs to match what you see in statements and paperwork. Even small mistakes here could signal issues to fix.

Look everything over for differences between your records and what the credit agency has on file. Reporting errors aren't uncommon, so speak up if you notice blips that ought to match up but don't.

Your credit report shapes many opportunities, so taking an hour now to review it more thoroughly could save you frustration later when it starts affecting things. A little prevention goes a long way.

CREATING A TARGETED PLAN FOR CREDIT REPAIR

You've taken the first big step by thoroughly reviewing your credit reports and understanding the key issues holding you back. Now it's time to map out a game plan for steadily improving your credit over the next year or so. Having that roadmap will help keep you focused and motivated through the process.

Start by making a list of all the negative items you need to address - things like unpaid collections, charge-offs, and late payments. Get all the details on balances owed, dates, and other relevant info. This will allow you to prioritize starting with the biggest, most damaging issues first.

For example, tackle the $15,000 defaulted auto loan that got charged off before worrying about an old $500 medical bill in collections. These big debts are like anchors weighing your credit down currently.

Once you've identified the highest priority items, you can start contacting creditors about making payment arrangements to settle or pay off the accounts. Don't be afraid to try negotiating a reduced payoff amount, especially on older debts with collection agencies. If you can afford to pay a decent lump sum upfront, you can sometimes settle for 50-70% of what was originally owed.

Even if you can't pay it all at once, setting up an installment plan to pay off the balances over several months is still progress in the right direction. Get it all in writing beforehand so there are no surprises down the line.

While you're chipping away at the big derogatory issues, stay current on minimum payments for open credit card accounts or loans you have. Paying all your bills on time is crucial.

If you have revolving accounts with high balances compared to the credit limit, call and request a credit limit increase after 6-12 months of on-time payments. This can significantly improve your credit utilization ratio, which is a big factor in your scores.

The key throughout this process is patience and discipline. Stick to your plan of systematically paying down debts, keeping balances low, and avoiding new late payments or delinquencies. Check your credit reports periodically to see derogatory items aging off and your scores improving from all your hard work.

It takes time, but staying dedicated to practicing good credit habits and responsibly rebuilding will get you to the point of having an excellent credit profile that opens up opportunities down the road. Don't get discouraged - permanent credit repair is a marathon, not a sprint. Stay the course, and it will pay off.

THE IMPORTANCE OF UNDERSTANDING DIFFERENT TYPES OF CREDIT INQUIRIES

Soft Searches

When credit card companies and loan brokers check your report to send you offers of pre-approvals, which are known as "soft inquiries." Soft searches are not directly tied to applications, so they barely cause a ripple in your credit report and score. Sometimes, you'll feel like you're getting rushes of spam mail after one soft check. However, rest assured, these won't do damage since they're sniffing around to target advertising.

Hard Pulls

Real applications for new credit accounts are marked as "hard inquiries" or "hard pulls" on your reports. Anytime you fill out a full application to take out a new loan, credit card, cell phone plan, or a new apartment, that runs a check known as a hard inquiry.

While one or two hard pulls over a year or two aren't too worrying and only affect your score a little, you do need to keep an eye on how many of these you get in a short period. Too many hard inquiries in a few months can look risky to lenders and make them question if you're gambling on more than you can chew. It's best to space loans and applications out when you can.

Prescreen Opt-Out

Sometimes, nosy companies you aren't doing business with will go ahead and run soft searches on your report without even getting your permission first. This is an annoying infringement. However, you have options to put a stop to it. One phone call opting out of "pre-screened" credit offers and the companies sending them won't be allowed to spy on your finances without cause. No more unwanted pre-approvals clogging your mailbox, either. Thus, take back control of your privacy when you notice such issues.

Checking Yourself

Any peeks you do at your report are perfectly fine. There's nothing wrong with keeping tabs. Nobody will penalize you for satisfying your curiosity. Catching mistakes early on is one perk, but you also get familiar with your numbers and payment patterns. Some outfits provide one of these complimentary checks once per year, so it's worth taking advantage of as part of staying informed.

KEY TAKEAWAYS

- Get your credit report from each big company - Experian, Equifax, TransUnion. Check for mistakes in your name, address, and accounts.
- Look at what types of accounts you have, such as credit cards, loans, or bills, and make sure they're all yours.
- Check whether you pay for everything on time. Late payments make scores drop fast, so pay attention.

- Lenders check your report when you apply for credit. Soft checks don't hurt, but hard checks lower scores a bit.
- Understanding where you're at now helps you make a plan to fix problems. If you see errors in your report, take action immediately.

In the next chapter, learn how to fix mistakes you might run into, such as late payments marked by accident or double accounts shown.

3

DISPUTING ERRORS ON YOUR CREDIT REPORT

M istakes on your credit report can unfairly hurt your score through no fault of your own. In this chapter, you'll learn common errors such as incorrect payment statuses, duplicate accounts, or wrong balances that may slip through. You have the right to dispute inaccuracies. The chapter will explain the dispute process step-by-step, like how to write a formal dispute letter and what supporting documents to include.

It's important to be detailed but concise when explaining the specific error. Be sure also to follow up if a credit bureau doesn't fix things in time. If a correction gets denied, this chapter will guide you on how to cover your options for further arguing your case with the bureaus or creditors directly. Taking extra time to check for errors and dispute them can go a long way in maintaining the best possible credit standing.

HOW ERRORS ON A CREDIT REPORT CAN LOWER CREDIT SCORES

Your credit scores are incredibly important numbers that can greatly shape your financial future. They determine whether you qualify for loans, credit cards, and rentals. Many people don't realize how significantly errors on their credit reports can drag credit scores down.

It's a simple equation - your credit scores are calculated directly from the information contained in your credit reports from major bureaus like Experian, Equifax, and TransUnion. If there are mistakes or inaccurate negative items listed on the reports, it's going to make your credit look worse than it is in reality. The miscalculations get baked into your scores.

Think of it like a teacher grading you incorrectly on an exam because they accidentally marked a number of your right answers as wrong. Through no fault of your own, your grade would suffer. The same thing happens with credit scores when there are errors in your credit report "answer key."

The impact can be staggering. Something as seemingly small as a single inaccurate 30-day late payment on your report could cause your scores to plummet by 100 points or more. That's like going from having excellent credit to poor credit overnight for no good reason! It's not only late payments - but negative items also that aren't truly yours can weigh your scores down like an anchor.

Maybe your credit report shows the wrong income or employment details, instantly making you look like a bigger risk to potential lenders. Perhaps it lists the same debt twice, doubling your apparent debt load and sky-high utilization ratio. Errors that make you look more leveraged and less able to afford your obligations are scoring kryptonite.

Even having too many unauthorized credit inquiries from companies pulling your report can inadvertently cause scoring damage. After all, the scoring models interpret a flurry of inquiries as someone desperate for new credit, despite it maybe being a case of identity fraud or wrongly assembled files.

The effects can be crippling as you get denied for apart-ments, mortgages, auto loans, credit lines - all because of someone else's errors that make you look unde-serving on paper. A single error might be the difference between getting approved with a great rate or outright rejection when buying that dream home.

It's a maddening and incredibly stressful situation that no consumer should have to endure, yet millions do each year. Honestly, thinking about having your scores unfairly dragged through the mud because of inaccurate information should be enough reason to scare you. Guarding and protecting your credit reputation from these errors needs to be a top priority.

These numbers can decide your entire financial roadmap and future opportunities. Thus, they need to be treated with the utmost care and accuracy at all times. Errors that turn your credit reputation upside down are simply unacceptable in this day and age. You deserve scores that are a true and foolproof reflection of your real-life financial standing and creditworthiness.

COMMON ERRORS oN CREDIT REPORTS

Incorrect Payment Status

Mistakes on credit reports showing late or missing payments can hurt your ability to get credit in the future. It is very important to carefully check the payment history and dispute errors. Small mistakes, like showing a payment as a week late when you paid on time, could cause problems later on. Lenders and companies you owe money to will look closely at your payment history when you apply for loans or credit, so mistakes need to be fixed.

It is smart to closely compare due dates and dates you made payments to records like bank statements. Report differences you find to the credit bureau. Payments marked as late or missing that your records show you made on or before the due date should not be reported that way. Since payment history affects your credit score, it is worth protecting an accurate payment record. Mistakes may stay on your report for long if not disputed, hurting your credit reputation for no good reason.

Taking time to carefully review each payment listed and check the info against bank records prevents small errors from becoming bigger issues. Even small, harmless mistakes could signal bigger underlying problems or start a pattern of less careful reporting. Catching errors early by closely monitoring your credit report is a good way to keep your credit profile clean and maximize future credit options. Thoroughly checking payment histories ensures only correct, verifiable information describes your financial history to lenders.

Duplicate Accounts

Seeing the same account or loan duplicated on your credit report when you only opened it once is an unnecessary mistake that needs to be fixed. Extra, unnecessary listings take up space but do not provide additional financial details to people reviewing your creditworthiness. Rather than help explain, duplicated accounts sow confusion and undermine the report's reliability through extra clutter.

Asking the reporting agency to combine duplicate entries helps streamline your credit report into an accurate, non-repetitive summary fitting its purpose. Lenders and creditors consider the number and types of accounts you have to evaluate creditworthiness, so repetition, where none is needed, may give an inaccurate impression different from reality. Duplicate listings also introduce more chances for discrepancies between entries to sneak in unnoticed if not reproduced identically in both instances.

Flagging and removing unnecessary repetitions maintains an organized credit report focused on the important details in a clear, easy-to-understand way. Extra or copied entries do not improve the information value of such an important personal financial record accessed by outside parties. Keeping your credit report concise and streamlined to only singular representations of each real account fosters transparency and fairness during reviews by potential new lenders or creditors.

Incorrect Account Balances

Reports showing amounts owed on accounts that are significantly different than your records require quick action to fix the mistakes. Large differences, whether balances are much higher or lower than truly owed, cause confusion and make it hard to understand your financial situation accurately. Lenders rely on accurate details in credit reports to properly understand your ability to repay debts.

Major purchases like cars, houses, or student loans listed with values much different than monthly statements undermine confidence in the reliability of all the information in your credit report. Listed balance amounts provide important signals about how much is still owed and the ability to responsibly manage credit use. Mistakes in reporting the usage and payment details run the risk of giving reviewers the wrong assessment and unfairly denying approval for future loans or available credit if not corrected.

With calendars and calculators in hand, carefully comparing all reported balance amounts to verifications from account statements and bills catches errors before harming your financial reputation and possibly leading to higher interest rates or denial of credit at a later time. Small mistakes may slip by overlooked, while large differences show the credit agency needs to properly update out-of-date or incorrect records using accurate information directly from your records. Maintaining clear records matched with regularly checking credit reports protects against flaws that could damage your creditworthiness.

Incorrectly Listed Accounts

Sometimes, old accounts remain on credit reports years after being paid off or closed, which does not follow normal timelines for removal. Also, some reports include accounts that were never opened at all, wrongly assuming you had financial obligations you did not have. Both of these issues require addressing problems.

Requesting the removal of incorrectly reported old accounts or suspected incorrect listings protects the accuracy and truthfulness of your financial history, which lenders can use to evaluate repayment risk now and in the future. Old or unlikely entries add clutter that could wrongly impact risk assessments if not properly checked.

Quickly disputing irrelevant items will make reports only include real, up-to-date accounts that are currently open or were closed according to standard timelines. Information that does not apply risks hiding the full picture that lenders need to review properly. Finding and fixing errors early by reviewing your records accurately reflects your current finances and past credit usage to be considered for new loans.

HOW TO DISPUTE INACCURACIES ON CREDIT REPORTS

It's important to check your credit report for mistakes. Your credit report tells lenders about how you paid bills in the past, like loans or credit cards. Lenders look at your report to see if they should lend you money or a credit card now.

That's why you need to check your report often and catch errors. Make sure the things listed happened.

The three big credit bureaus are Experian, Equifax, and TransUnion. When you find a mistake, contact each bureau with the wrong information. Tell them what's wrong. You'll need to show proof, too. Here's how to dispute inaccuracies:

Write a Dispute Letter

Write a letter to the bureau about the mistake. Be clear about which part is wrong. Maybe things like the name, phone number, and date of birth. Keep it short, but include all details.

Send Documentation

Send copies of papers that support you, like bank papers, bills, receipts, and letters to the company. Send copies, not the real papers. The more proof, the better chance to fix it. Include the papers with your letter.

Send to the Right Address

Make sure to mail your letter and copies to the legal address for disputes, not the regular one. You want it to go through the right process. The addresses are online or in your reports. Contact each bureau separately.

Follow the Process

Some disputes are resolved quickly, but others may be difficult. If they refuse to fix something you know is wrong, stay polite but firm. You can add a brief statement. As a last option, file a complaint.

Dispute Creditors Too

Sometimes, mistakes on your credit report involve errors made directly by the original creditors, like banks, credit card companies, utility providers, or other lenders. In these situations, credit bureaus may be unable to correct the problems themselves since they report what information creditors gave them. That's why it's also important to dispute inaccuracies directly with the creditors holding the accounts in question.

The first step is to identify which accounts on your credit report contain inaccurate information you want to dispute. Take note of details like the account name, number, and date. Then, locate contact information for the specific creditor. Most provide a mailing address for disputes on their website or statements. You can also try calling their customer service line to be connected to the right department.

When contacting the creditor, remain polite but firm. Explain that you've identified incorrect information reporting to the credit bureaus regarding your account. Provide brief details to identify the specific issue. For instance, you may say, "I am writing to dispute an inaccurate late payment that was reported for April 2024. I have records showing my payment was made on time that month."

It's a good idea to include documentation supporting your side of the dispute, like when challenging errors with the credit bureaus. Copies of statements, receipts, or correspondence are useful for demonstrating proof the creditor's records contain mistakes. You can scan and email documents if the creditor accepts electronic disputes or mail hard copies if not.

Remember to include your name, address, account number, the last four digits of your Social Security number, and other verifying details the creditor may need to properly identify your account. As required by federal law, request a response or result of the investigation within 30 days.

Be prepared to escalate your dispute if the initial creditor contact doesn't help resolve the issue promptly. First, follow up politely but persistently if you don't receive a response within the requested time frame. You can call, email, or send a certified letter noting your previous correspondence and asking for an update.

If the creditor still denies inaccuracies after reviewing your supporting documentation, consider obtaining management assistance. Request to speak or write directly to a supervisor or manager. Remain respectful while stressing the importance of correcting mistaken information harming your credit profile. Keep detailed notes of all contact attempts, dates, and responses for records. As a last resort, you can submit a complaint to the Consumer Financial Protection Bureau.

Mistakes happen, but following these steps will fix inaccuracies. Regular checks allow you to catch problems sooner for faster solutions. With accuracy, your true history and ability will be clear.

What to Do If a Dispute Is Denied

You put a lot of effort into fixing mistakes on your credit reports, but sometimes creditors or the credit bureaus don't see it your way. They might flat-out deny that errors exist despite the proof you provided. It's frustrating, but don't give up - you still have options to straighten things out.

First, go over the denial carefully. Look at what policies or records they're using to justify keeping the current information. Getting a clear picture of where they're coming from may help guide your next move. If there's a payment recording mix-up, added clarification could potentially resolve it.

No matter if the denial comes from a creditor or the credit bureau itself, you have the right to add a short statement to your report explaining your side. Write up to 100 words outlining the key points and why you still firmly believe there's an error. Stick to the relevant facts without going off on tangents. That statement then gets attached anytime that disputed item gets looked at.

You can also try re-submitting the dispute with new supporting documentation you've managed to dig up. Sometimes, additional proof surfaces that can nail down your case. Don't be afraid to go directly to the creditor and request old statements, letters, receipts - whatever might help build your case. Leave no stone unturned in searching for the golden evidence.

If you're hitting a brick wall no matter what you submit, it may be time to escalate things to higher-ups. Politely but firmly call or email supervisors and consumer relations staff asking for a re-review. As intimidating as it seems, a courteous yet firm approach often leads to an actual fresh set of eyes on your dispute. Be sure to follow up on denials in writing to create a paper trail.

When re-submitting disputes, update them with new angles or evidence you've found. Reference the paper trail of previous attempts. Sometimes, refreshing your reasoning and supplementing with new proof is what finally resolves a dispute after earlier failed attempts. Persistence does pay off when done respectfully.

If you've tried every internal channel and creditors are downright unreasonable about a legitimate grievance, you can file complaints with outside organizations like the Consumer Financial Protection Bureau or FTC. Include your full documentation trail - these impartial parties can help mediate a resolution.

As a last resort, you may need to consult a consumer lawyer about potential litigation over clear-cut errors that are severely damaging your finances or reputation unfairly. Small claims court can sometimes be the most efficient way to resolve open-and-shut cases. Lawsuits are the nuclear option after all diplomatic routes have failed.

While denied disputes are incredibly frustrating, the power to correct your credit record is still in your hands through persistent yet polite efforts. Removing inaccuracies preserves your good credit reputation and protects you from mistreatment due to bad data. Stay determined but also reasonable - consumer diligence truly does lead to fair outcomes when you assert your rights thoughtfully.

KEY TAKEAWAYS

- Mistakes in your report, such as wrong payment information, can hurt your score.
- Common errors are late marks for on-time payments and duplicate accounts.
- You can send a dispute letter or use the online form to explain what's wrong. If you received it, include proof.
- Be patient - the credit bureaus have a month to check it out. Follow up if they don't reply.

- If the error is from the lender, contact them to have it fixed. Keep pushing until it's solved.

Setting financial goals takes planning. Continue reading to learn how crafting an effective credit repair strategy can help make your aspirations a reality.

4

DEVELOPING A CREDIT REPAIR PLAN

This chapter will discuss creating a plan to improve your credit score. Making a strategy is important since credit repair takes effort, and it helps you stay organized. First, the chapter will cover setting realistic goals based on your situation. Don't try to fix everything at once. From there, the chapter will show how to map out a timeline to reach each objective step-by-step.

It's also key to have a budget to help tackle debts. Don't worry if it seems complicated now. The chapter provides examples of well-thought-out plans that make the process easier to follow. Having a clear path reduces the stress of fixing your credit. You'll also learn how to track your progress so you stay motivated. Your goals may change as life happens, so you'll learn how to adjust plans as needed. By creating an effective repair blueprint, you'll be well-equipped to improve your credit score in less than a year.

THE IMPORTANCE OF HAVING AN EFFECTIVE CREDIT REPAIR PLAN

Anytime you apply for a loan, credit card, mortgage, or renting an apartment, lenders and creditors are going to scrutinize your credit report and score. If your credit score is in the gutter, be ready for rejections, sky-high interest rates, and getting stuck with terrible deals. To lenders, a low score makes you look like a huge risk, so they do everything possible to cover themselves - even if it means making credit absurdly expensive and hard to get when you need it most.

What if you maintain a good credit profile? That's your golden ticket to access better opportunities and save yourself a fortune. You get the best rates and terms on loans, mortgages, and credit cards - potentially tens of thousands in savings over the life of the accounts. A stellar credit report signals you're a rock-solid, responsible borrower deserving of premium offers.

Why You Need a Solid Credit Repair Plan

If your credit isn't looking too good, don't panic. You can turn things around in less than a year. However, repairing damaged credit takes consistent hard work over months, not an overnight magic fix. That's precisely why having a comprehensive, strategic game plan is crucial from the start.

Without a clear, well-mapped-out roadmap, it's too easy to get lost, overwhelmed, and maybe inadvertently make mistakes that worsen your credit further. A carefully thought-out plan keeps you laser-focused and organized, ensuring you knock out your biggest problem areas first for maximum impact on your scores.

The Key Plan Components

An effective, comprehensive credit repair plan includes certain essential items. Here's what you should incorporate:

Understanding Your Full Reports

First, get current copies of your full credit reports from the three major bureaus: Experian, Equifax, and Trans-Union. Comb through every line item carefully, noting inaccuracies, errors, or negative entries that seem bogus and unfairly stain your record.

Prioritizing Your Efforts

With a clear picture of what you're dealing with, prioritize which issues to tackle based on what's dragging your credit scores down the hardest and what'll be easiest to resolve. Most likely, that means going scorched earth on major blemishes like unpaid collections and charge-offs first.

Structuring Payment Plans

For legitimate outstanding debts you have to deal with, work on setting up payment plans, or try to negotiate reduced settlements. Having a structured payment schedule will keep you disciplined and making steady progress toward resolving problematic accounts.

Disputing Errors and Inaccuracies

If you catch outright errors or inaccurate negative items, dispute them immediately with the relevant credit bureaus. Getting the incorrect information removed from your file could instantly boost your score.

Reducing Credit Utilization

Your credit utilization ratio - how much combined balance you're carrying versus your total credit limits - is another huge scoring factor. Look for ways to lower this ratio, like making payments towards balances or requesting credit limit increases.

Tracking Your Progress

This won't be a short journey, so get used to routinely checking your credit reports and scores to monitor your progress.

The Payoff Is Huge

Your credit report and score hold immense power over many areas of your financial present and future. Having a comprehensive, strategic repair plan lets you regain control and pave the way toward an elite credit profile that opens up a world of opportunities.

HOW TO SET REALISTIC CREDIT GOALS

When repairing or building up your credit, setting realistic goals is crucial. Having overly ambitious targets is setting yourself up for disappointment. That's why tailoring your credit goals to your unique financial situation is so important.

Take a look at where you're starting from. What range is your current credit score sitting in? What kinds of negative garbage like missed payments and collections are weighing you down? Getting a clear picture of your present credit profile lays the foundation for establishing goals you can achieve.

For example, if several collection accounts are dragging you down with a score trapped in the 550 poor range, then setting a goal to hit an 800+ score within 6 months is delusional. A more reasonable short-term target might be aiming to go your way up in the 650-675 range by resolving the collections and establishing a steady, on-time payment history.

Your income level and other existing debt you're juggling factor heavily into what kinds of credit goals make sense for you to set right now, too. If money is extremely tight, then an overly aggressive paydown plan for all your revolving balances might not be feasible. Setting a realistic goal of simply maintaining minimum payments to avoid new delinquencies could be the smarter move.

The key is finding a sweet spot to balance your aspirations with pragmatism based on your current life circumstances. Shoot for incremental, achievable goals that meaningfully improve your credit situation gradually without becoming so lofty that you inevitably get demotivated and give up before ever reaching them.

Creating a Roadmap with Milestones

Once you set realistic short- and long-term credit goals tailored to your current financial standing, it's time to create a clear roadmap for systematically reaching the targets.

Start by breaking down your overarching goals into bite-sized milestone achievements to work towards sequentially. These milestones serve as motivating checkpoints along your full credit repair journey.

Assume your first big goal is increasing your credit score to 650 within the next 12 months by paying off collections and catching up on past-due accounts you have. You could set incremental milestones like:

- **3 Months:** Settle and pay off the smallest collection account. Score increase: +25 pts
- **6 Months:** Settle and pay off the largest collection account. Score increase: +40 pts
- **9 Months:** All past due accounts are now current, making payments as agreed. Score increase: +35 pts
- **12 Months:** Finally reached the initial 650-score goal!

From there, you can establish a new long-term goal, such as aiming for a 720+ score to qualify for the best interest rates and loan terms. Set milestones for steps like reducing your overall credit utilization below 30%, increasing credit limits on current cards or lines, and maintaining an extended period of super positive payment history.

These sequential milestones create a mapped-out path of steps to follow, with built-in progress check-ins that keep you motivated all along the way. You'll know how far you've come towards your ultimate goals and what hurdles are left to clear.

Realistic credit goals combined with a clear roadmap allow you to stay motivated and make sustainable progress toward the lasting credit revival you're after. Setting the bar too high and failing miserably does nothing but drain your morale. Stay grounded and stick to your plan, and your credit score will rise steadily.

HOW TO ESTABLISH A BUDGET TO MANAGE AND REDUCE DEBT

Dealing with debt and bad credit can feel like a nightmare. It's easy to get overwhelmed and want to stick your head in the sand. However, what makes this whole process more manageable? Having a solid monthly budget locked in is the best way out.

With a clear spending plan, you'll know where every dollar is going each month and where you can cut back to free up cash for debt payments.

The first thing to do is gather your latest bills, statements, and paycheck stubs—anything showing your income and expenses. From there, separate everything into basic necessity categories like rent or mortgage, utilities, groceries, car payments and insurance, and minimum debt payments you're already making.

Once you have these essentials covered, take a good look at your "wants" spending, such as dining out, entertainment, subscriptions, and memberships. You'll likely spot a few non-essential expenses you can reduce or temporarily eliminate to divert more money towards chipping away at debt.

Trimming Expenses and Budgeting Windfalls

Once you've created your new budgeting blueprint for allocating income toward necessities and debt payments each month, you need to stick to it.

Look for more ways to cut back on discretionary spending and divert the savings towards paying off debt faster. Check if you can downgrade things like cable TV packages or internet plans. Negotiate bills like your cell phone or insurance rates. Cut out subscription services and memberships you rarely use.

Also, cook more meals at home instead of constantly ordering out, which can add up quickly. If your schedule allows you to generate extra money to pay off debt, you could pick up a short-term side gig or temporary job.

When little windfalls like tax refunds, work bonuses, or gift money from relatives or friends come your way, budget as much of this money as possible towards your debt freedom plan instead of splurging it on fun. These lump-sum amounts can accelerate your payoff date.

Budgeting is all about purposely deciding where every dollar goes each month. Once you have a system for tracking spending and making strategic debt payments, that seemingly insurmountable debt mountain will no longer feel so scary and overwhelming.

The Importance of Tracking Your Progress

By now, you have worked hard to map out a solid plan for repairing your credit, establishing a budget to crush debt, and setting up a roadmap with clear milestones. Now comes the crucial part of consistently tracking your progress to ensure that all that effort isn't going to waste.

Trying to repair your credit without closely monitoring how you're progressing is like embarking on a cross-country road trip without a map or GPS. Sure, you might eventually stumble across your destination, but you're going to get lost a million times, waste gas on unnecessary detours, and show up way later than needed. That is not an ideal scenario, right?

By routinely checking your latest credit reports and scores, you can see what items are getting resolved, how your payment histories are shaping up, and whether your credit utilization percentages are trending in the right direction. These insights confirm if your grand plan is working as intended and if you're still on pace to hit the target milestones you outlined.

Staying Motivated

One of the biggest upsides to tracking your credit repair progress religiously is the motivation it provides for sticking to your plan through the inevitable rough patches. Rebuilding your credit profile from scratch takes serious time and effort over many months - it's only natural to occasionally feel frustrated or want to slack off.

What if you check your reports and score to find you've steadily gone from a 580 to a 620 over the past few months as you knocked out collections? Or what if a maxed-out credit card you've been chipping away at is now down to a healthier 30% utilization? These tangible wins, no matter how small, remind you that your plan and disciplined approach are paying dividends.

It's validating to see real progress after all your hard work. These feel-good moments make it easier to power through when debt payments start feeling tedious or other aspects of executing your plan hit an inevitable lull.

Adjusting Your Approach When Needed

Even the most carefully thought-out credit repair strategy won't be set in stone forever. Things change - maybe you land a new job with a higher income that frees up more money for accelerated debt payments, or an unexpected financial emergency comes up that forces you to temporarily scale back how aggressively you can attack debts.

That's why it's crucial to consistently track your progress and overall financial situation each month. Doing that allows you to identify when your original plan needs adjusting to remain realistic and achievable based on your current circumstances.

There's no sense sticking to a debt payment schedule or timeline that's grown outdated or unrealistic for your life as it exists today. You've got to stay nimble and ready to adapt and pivot your approach as needed. Modify payment amounts, delay certain milestones if cash is tight, or double down and accelerate others if your finances improve.

Using your progress tracking to perform regular honest check-ins on whether your credit repair roadmap is still setting you up for sustainable, lasting success. Make calculated adjustments, don't get deterred by temporary setbacks, and keep the vision of an elite credit profile in focus.

Diligently monitoring your progress keeps you motivated, confirms when your hard work is paying off, and allows you to course-correct. It's what separates successful, strategic credit rebuilding efforts from aimless attempts doomed to fail before ever gaining traction.

KEY TAKEAWAYS

- Making a credit repair plan helps you fix your credit in a way that works for your money and life.
- Target small wins like paying one bill extra each month before moving to bigger goals.
- Schedule goals so you know what to focus on monthly.
- Map out a budget to free up cash for debts and start saving.

- Check how you're doing along the way so you can tweak your plan and keep going forward.

Managing debt is key to better credit. The next chapter offers tips on paying it off strategically through balance transfers and negotiating with creditors.

5

PAYING DOWN DEBT STRATEGICALLY

Getting a handle on your existing debts is an important part of strengthening your credit. This chapter looks into strategies for managing what you owe in a thoughtful, organized way. The chapter will compare the "debt snowball" and "debt avalanche" methods, which are two popular approaches to chipping away at balances one by one. Next, you'll find tips for paying extra toward loans with nagging high interest rates and seeing if creditors will meet you halfway with more favorable terms.

Managing credit cards prudently makes a difference, too, like sticking to a budget and not missing payments. With a systematic debt repayment plan, you can gradually reduce your debt while simultaneously helping your credit score climb. The chapter will also cover preventive measures, such as focusing on your long-term goals to avoid new debt and using balance transfers intelligently if needed.

WHY MANAGING DEBT IS CRITICAL IN IMPROVING CREDIT SCORE

One of the biggest killers of solid credit scores is unmanaged debt. Debts you can't handle weigh down your credit.

Maybe you're dealing with maxed-out credit cards where you're paying minimums each month and never putting a dent in the principal. Perhaps old medical bills, personal loans, or utility debts fell into collections because things spiraled beyond your control.

Whatever the specifics, accumulating debt without a plan for systematically paying it off is financial death for your credit scores. The delinquent accounts, charge-offs ending up in collections, and consistently sky-high credit utilization ratios demolish your credit numbers into oblivion.

It Creates a Vicious Downward Spiral

The frustrating part is that unmanaged debt creates a vicious, self-perpetuating downward spiral that gets tougher to escape. As your scores tank from a mountain of derogatory debt items, getting approved for potential new credit or loans that could help provide financial breathing room becomes harder.

With less ability to open new credit sources that could dilute your utilization, you're forced to lean more heavily on maxing out existing credit lines to stay afloat. That only leads to higher utilization percentages and more missed payments getting marked as delinquent.

Before long, your total debt load has snowballed out of control while your credit scores plummet to unimaginable levels. This closes off more lending avenues that could help get out of everything. It's a soul-crushing, anxiety-inducing spiral that's way too easy for anyone to slip into without a plan in place.

Laying Out a Strategic Repayment Plan

With all the harsh realities in mind, it should be obvious why getting a structured debt management and repayment plan in place needs to be your top priority. It's necessary if improving your credit score is the goal.

Start by laying out your current debts and their pertinent details - total balance owed, interest rates, current minimum monthly payments, and delinquency statuses. A full picture lets you decide which repayment strategy works best for your unique income and cash flow situation. Maybe it's the classic debt snowball of knocking out the smallest balances first or the debt avalanche approach taking care of the highest interest rates upfront.

From there, make a realistic monthly budget that allocates as much disposable income as possible to systematically chip away at debt based on your established priorities. Finding small ways to trim recurring monthly expenses further or picking a temporary side gig to generate supplemental debt payment money helps.

The key is steadily reducing the burdensome debt obligations instead of raising interest fees. As the balances are paid down, previously worrisome credit utilization ratios start improving in your favor. Clearing out delinquencies or settling charged-off collection accounts gives your scores an extra upward nudge in the right direction.

Stay Dedicated

After making a few payments, recovering from significant debt, and fully repairing your credit profile doesn't happen overnight. It's a marathoner's game that requires serious dedication and perseverance over many months to see it through to the finish line.

You're going to hit low points along the way where you feel burned out, demoralized, or frustrated by the seemingly glacial progress that's happening despite all your hard work and budgeting efforts. That's why tracking your credit reports and scores consistently is crucial to spot hard-fought victories. The little milestone wins provide valuable bursts of motivation to power through the grind.

You also have to be mentally prepared to adjust your repayment plans and budgets when needed as your income or expense situation shifts. Don't get thrown off the track or deterred by temporary setbacks, either. In such instances, pause, reassess your approach, and get back after it.

Maintaining a big-picture mindset focused on the potential that an excellent revitalized credit score opens up - from better mortgage and loan rates to easily securing the nicest rental properties and scoring the cheapest insurance premiums.

HOW TO PRIORITIZE HIGH-INTEREST DEBTS AND NEGOTIATE FOR BETTER TERMS

Prioritizing High-Interest Debts

The first step is taking stock of all your debts and interest rates. Pull out recent statements from all your credit cards, personal loans, and other forms of borrowing you have. This can be an eye-opening experience, so be prepared. Make a list with the name of each lender and your current balance, minimum payment, and interest rate for each debt.

Once you have everything written down, it's time to sort your debts from highest to lowest interest rate. Debts with rates over 20% should be at the top of your priority list. These are probably credit cards you've had for a long time and accrued a balance. The interest is piling up on these debts monthly.

It's a good idea to calculate how much extra you are paying in interest alone on these high-interest-rate cards compared to your lower-rate debts. To do this, look at the interest charged over the last 3-6 months on each debt. Subtracting the minimum payments from the total interest will show how much is added to your balances. You may be surprised by how the numbers add up fast.

Knowing these dollar amounts can help motivate you to stay on track and pay off high-rate debts as fast as possible. Even making a $20-50 payment toward the top card weekly in addition to minimums can knock it out much sooner. As one high-rate debt falls, you can roll the extra payment amount to the next highest-rate card to snowball your progress.

Negotiating with Creditors for Better Terms

With your debts organized, it's time to start making friendly contact with each creditor. Pick up the phone and call the customer service line listed on the statement during business hours. Explain that you've fallen into financial difficulties due to reasons like a lost job, medical bills, or family issues, but you're dedicated to paying off all obligations.

Request to speak to a representative and ask politely if they have options available to reduce your interest rate by a few percentage points. Many creditors have programs for rate reductions or temporary hardship plans in certain situations. Be prepared to provide proof of your hardship if asked, such as pay stubs, medical bills, or bank statements. Don't forget your manners - saying please and thank you will get you further.

If rate reductions are not available, ask about transferring balances to cards offering an introductory 0% APR period, often 6-18 months. This can save a lot on interest if you pay off the full transfer amount before the low rate expires. However, be aware of balance transfer fees, which are about 3-5% of the transfer amount, so only do this if committed to paying it off quickly. Keep records of agreements so there are no surprises down the road.

Finally, see if minimum payments can be lowered temporarily if needed. While this extends your payoff timeline, every little bit helps if money is extremely tight. The goal is to keep your accounts in good standing so you can maintain access to future credit as your situation improves. Don't hesitate to call back if initial attempts don't provide relief. Sometimes, a different representative may have alternate options.

Managing Credit Card Debt Effectively

Now that you've organized debts and contacted lenders, it's time for a budget overhaul to manage card balances properly going forward. Start by writing down all your monthly income from jobs, financial assistance, or other sources. Be realistic – don't overestimate.

Next, list all essential monthly expenses—housing, utilities, food, transportation, and minimum debt payments. Add in daily spending amounts for estimated personal and household needs. Your goal is to cut overall costs as much as possible to free up extra cash for debt repayment. Consider lowering cable packages, cell phone plans, or other discretionary expenses first.

Now you have the full picture of inflows and outflows. Money remaining after expenses should be applied in addition to the highest-interest credit card debt. The snowball method pays off - you'll begin to see balances slowly fall, which creates positive motivation to keep going.

There may be months with unexpected bills that prevent larger than minimum debt payments. As long as you stay focused on reducing spending and living below your means, progress will happen. Small steps each month of paying a little above minimum add up towards becoming debt-free.

Most importantly, credit cards should only be used for absolute necessities if balances are still outstanding. Watch statements like a hawk for errors and pay the statement balance in full each month if able to avoid interest completely. Even paying a few months' interest charges can reduce your balance much faster. Be persistent - you have the power to turn things around in less than a year.

HOW TO REDUCE DEBT BURDEN THROUGH STRATEGIC DEBT REPAYMENT

You can climb out from a suffocating debt burden by taking a thoughtful, strategic approach to repayment.

Why a Strategic Plan Matters

Making the minimum payment on all your debts each month may seem like the easiest short-term solution.

However, this is the slowest, most painful way to try getting out. Without a well-constructed plan for prioritizing payments, you'll end up pouring a lot of money down the drain in interest charges. It's a vicious cycle that can leave you feeling trapped indefinitely.

The smart move is getting strategic about which debts you attack first and how much extra you can dump toward them each month. With a clear, properly executed payoff plan in place, you'll make progress and see results faster. The high-interest balances will start melting away as you gain invaluable financial traction. Best of all, you'll wave goodbye to the anxiety sooner by becoming debt-free.

TWO PROVEN REPAYMENT METHODS

The Debt Snowball

One of the most popular debt payoff strategies is the snowball method. With this approach, you'll list out all your various debts from the smallest current balance to the largest, regardless of their interest rates.

Then, you'll make the minimum payment as usual on every single debt except the smallest one. For that smallest balance, you'll throw extra money toward paying it off at a rapid pace. Once the first debt is demolished, you'll take the amount you were paying on it and roll it over to the next smallest balance. This allows you to make a bigger payment toward the debt.

The strategy continues with you paying minimums on everything else while dedicating a growing "snowball" toward whichever debt is now the smallest. As each balance gets paid off one by one, you apply the previous payments to the next debt. This efficient debt stacking allows the snowball to grow more massive with every cremated debt, helping you mow them all down faster.

The key psychological benefit of the debt snowball is that clearing your smallest debts first can provide a motivating burst of momentum. This positive reinforcement often helps people stick to the payoff plan long-term.

The Debt Avalanche

If you're a math person who wants to optimize to save the most money on interest, the debt avalanche method may be preferable. This strategy involves listing out all your debts from highest interest rate to lowest, regardless of their current balance amounts.

You'll continue making minimum payments on every single debt, like with the snowball approach. But this time, you'll attack the debt with the highest annual percentage rate (APR) first by throwing as much extra money as possible toward its outstanding principal balance each month. Once that highest-interest debt is paid off, you'll roll over everything you were paying toward your next highest-interest balance.

On the surface, the avalanche can feel less satisfying than demolishing a bunch of smaller debts right away. This method allows you to efficiently eliminate the debts costing you the most in interest charges. While it may take longer to see your first debt cleared, sticking to the avalanche yields the biggest savings and fastest payoff timeframe.

If mathematical optimization isn't a huge priority and you're more motivated by small psychological wins, the snowball might be preferable. However, if you can stay disciplined and want to save as much as possible on interest, the debt avalanche tends to be the superior strategy.

CREATING YOUR PAYOFF PLAN

Now that you understand two of the most effective, proven methods for chipping away at debt from a position of systematic strength, it's time to get rolling on executing your payoff plan the right way.

Whichever repayment strategy you select, make sure to lay it out visually to provide transparency in your plan. Create a spreadsheet or list that shows your debts in the appropriate order based on whether you're snow-balling or doing an avalanche. Calculate how much you'll need to pay toward the top debt each month over the minimum to make satisfactory progress.

Next, look at where you can free enough cash flow to make the elevated debt payments possible. Could you cut costs elsewhere in your monthly budget, such as scaling back subscriptions, gym memberships, dining out, or other non-essential expenses? Is there an oppor-tunity to pick up a part-time job for extra income? Maybe you get an annual bonus from your employer that you can commit to putting toward debt repayment each year.

You need to get creative about spending as much extra money as possible beyond your regular bills and basic living expenses. The bigger the payments you can make toward your targeted debt, the faster you'll pay it off and expedite your overall debt-free mission.

Staying Motivated

Whenever you feel your commitment starting to waver, take a step back. Remind yourself why you decided to finally get serious about strategically repaying debt:

- To stop constantly stressing about making ends meet each month.

- To improve your poor credit score and qualify for better rates.
- To free up cash for investing toward other priorities like saving for retirement.
- To gain true control of your finances and build lasting wealth.

Plaster motivational images, quotes, or debt payoff trackers somewhere you'll see often to stay inspired. Dedicate the money you would've wasted on interest to invest in yourself instead through books, courses, or experiences.

Most importantly, keep focused on the immense freedom and relief you'll feel once the last debt is cleared.

TIPS FOR AVOIDING NEW DEBT

Living within Your Means

Making sure your expenses are less than your income is one of the best things you can do to avoid new debt. Take a close look at what's coming in and what's going out each month to see where you have room to save a little here and there.

Start by writing down the amount you earn from your job and other money that's contributing to your income. Be realistic about what you can expect. It's better to underestimate than be disappointed.

Then, go through your bills like rent or mortgage, utilities, food, transportation, insurance, and minimum loan payments. Also, estimate what you're spending on gas, eating out, fun activities, and personal spending. Check past statements from the last few months to get a good idea of your average costs.

As you compare money in versus money out, look for ways to trim discretionary spending. Maybe you can find a cheaper place to live or a cell phone plan. Cooking more meals at home instead of eating out can save a bundle, too. Canceling streaming subscriptions or memberships for a while may free up a little cash. After paying for needs, extra money should go towards existing debt.

The goal is for your income to be more than what you need each month. That protects you in case of unexpected repairs or medical bills instead of putting them on a credit card with interest. Keeping close track of where your money goes is key to finding places to cut back and keeping expenses below what you earn.

Build an Emergency Fund

Having savings stashed away for unplanned costs is helpful for avoiding going further into debt when life throws curveballs. An emergency fund acts as a financial safety net besides credit cards to handle surprises.

You can start with $500 to $1,000 in your emergency fund savings and add to it until you have 3 to 6 months' worth of essential expenses covered. Even small contributions each paycheck can make a difference if you keep at it.

In the beginning, putting together a rainy day fund from nothing may feel slow. But every little bit counts —it all adds up eventually. Look for $20-50 a month you can divert from discretionary spending into your special savings account. Consistently doing that for a year can yield $240 to $600 without too much pain.

Once you have emergency cash built up, only dip into it when there's truly no other choice. Let it grow so it's there for car repairs, medical bills, or whatever life throws your way, so you're not forced to rely on using credit cards and paying interest. Even a small cushion will reduce stress during rough patches. With commitment, this reserve fund will keep you protected from future debt problems.

Use Cards Wisely

Many people these days find it hard to completely avoid credit cards. However, it's important to use them in a smart way to prevent running up new card balances and high-interest charges. Here are strategies that can help keep plastic from causing more debt trouble down the road:

- Set a monthly credit card spending limit and stick to it. Look at past statements to realistically decide what you can afford to pay off each month while still throwing extras at existing loans.
- Keep close tabs on all purchases so nothing slips through the cracks. You may find it easier to use cash instead of cards whenever possible.
- Never let payments roll over to the next month, where interest starts accruing. Always pay at least the full statement balance on time to avoid slipping backward.
- Watch for credit limit increases and consider asking for lower caps if you have trouble restraining near-maxed-out levels.

With diligence and proper management, cards can help build a positive payment record instead of drowning you in compounding interest charges. This takes self-control but will keep your finances sailing smoothly going forward.

KEY TAKEAWAYS

- Getting a plan to knock out debt is a crucial part of credit repair.
- Two main strategies are snowball (focus small bills first for faster wins) or avalanche (highest interests come down quickest).
- Call card companies and request lower rates to make payments more helpful.
- Use cards only for essentials while paying more than the minimum each month.
- Think hard before taking out new debt, like 0% transfers, which expire fast. One slip can cost a lot in interest.

Building a strong credit history requires dedication. The next chapter uncovers key tactics for getting your financial history in order.

6

BUILDING POSITIVE CREDIT HISTORY

I n this chapter, you'll learn why it's important to have good, positive information on your credit reports. Making all your bill payments on time is key to a high score. The chapter will discuss how much you charge to different accounts. The chapter explains options like secured cards that can help build your history.

Becoming an authorized user or taking out an installment loan can also add good factors to your file. This chapter will look at how developing a solid record of on-time repayment helps your score. You'll also get tips here for keeping credit utilization low and balancing the kinds of accounts reported. Following these steps will put you in a great place to maintain excellent credit.

IMPORTANCE OF A POSITIVE CREDIT HISTORY

A Good History Means Better Options

Your credit history follows you for many years and directly impacts the financial opportunities available to you. When you apply for loans, mortgages, credit cards, or many rental properties, one of the first places lenders will look is your credit reports. They want to understand how reliably you've paid your debts and obligations in the past.

Past instances of late or missed payments, accounts sent to collections, liens, bankruptcies, or other negative items will cause your credit scores to drop significantly. This not only lowers your approval odds but triggers much worse loan terms if approved. Interest rates on extended credit will be much higher to offset the added risk from a spotty record.

On the other hand, demonstrating a long-term pattern of making all payments on time every single month shows lenders that you are a low-risk, trusted borrower. This consistency results in higher credit scores, allowing you greater access to favorable financing options down the road. You'll qualify for competitive mortgage rates or auto loans at lower annual percentage rates.

Your credit activity right now of diligently keeping accounts in good standing translates directly to the kinds of choices and opportunities available to take advantage of later in life. Something as simple as needing a small credit limit increase on a card or wanting to finance a reliable used vehicle - you'll be in a prime position to get approved. A perfect record of responsibility leads to greater eligibility for building home equity or pursuing an advanced degree program years from now, too, when life's milestones arrive.

Avoid Costly Penalties

The immediate downside of missed loan payments goes beyond hurting your credit scores—lenders will initiate charges and consequences when bills fall delinquent. Late fees, typically ranging from $25 to $40, are common for credit cards or personal loans not paid on schedule. The longer amounts stay unpaid, the higher the additional penalties.

More serious ramifications involve persistent lateness, affecting terms of future credit needed. Auto or mortgage approvals may happen but at elevated interest rates, factoring in higher perceived default risk. Interest charged on revolving credit lines and future loans will be markedly higher, costing borrowers thousands of extra dollars.

Beyond facing disapproval, those with damaged credit histories pay a premium to borrow money. Financial institutions genuinely prefer customers exhibiting solid habits and keeping accounts current and active. Clean records identify individuals likely to meet their responsibilities monthly. Your dedicated attention prevents ever suffering unnecessary charges or ongoing added costs due to a history of troubles fulfilling obligations properly.

Punctuality maintains satisfactory relationships with lenders and protects your funds. Responsible management minimizes out-of-pocket penalties while sustaining desirability, taking advantage of affordable loan choices down the road for bigger life needs or unexpected circumstances like vehicle repairs without stressing finances. A little effort now spares much future burden.

IMPORTANCE OF MAKING TIMELY PAYMENTS AND USING CREDIT RESPONSIBLY

Pay Now, Benefit Later

Making timely payments on your financial obligations is one of the most important things you can do for your financial future. When bills are paid in full and on schedule each month, it shows lenders that you are a low-risk and responsible borrower. This consistency is what allows your credit scores to remain high.

The benefits of paying go beyond protecting your scores. Meeting payment deadlines means avoiding costly late fees that can erase savings from bills. Late charges typically range from $25-40 per loan or credit card, adding up fast if lapses continue. Being dutiful prevents wasting hard-earned money.

Strong credit scores attained through years of dutiful, timely payments will directly translate to lower-interest financing. When future needs for a vehicle, property, or education funding arise, and credit approval is required, solid scores will position you for the most competitive loan rates available. Even trimming 1% off a 30-year home mortgage by qualifying for the best terms can reduce total payment amounts by thousands of dollars.

When you establish a proven track record, you gain the upper hand during important credit applications. Personal loans, auto refinancing, and 0% balance transfer cards will all have lower costs, with pristine payment histories backing the applications.

Act Responsibly, Stay in Control

Proper credit management demands self-discipline in only borrowing judiciously for needs while avoiding the dangers of revolving plastic debt carrying high-interest fees. Strategic card use means planning to pay statement balances fully each month from available cash flows. This prevents dollars spent from morphing into much pricier dollar amounts owed through compounding rate charges.

For debts you're unable to pay off immediately, committing to more than minimums aims to gradually shrink what's owed quicker. Being dogged about whittling larger sums down faster protects from getting buried by accruing interest costs ballooning out of control. Constant vigilance in monitoring expenses and debt levels maintains the upper hand feeling in command of financial affairs rather than being controlled by them.

Self-imposed spending ceilings keep leverage by avoiding credit line increases, tempting overextension. Discipline withstands marketing ploys trying to normalize unneeded purchases at 30% APRs.

Prudently rationing credit access for unavoidable costs alone establishes positive payment records for future requests. Handling obligations responsibly secures favorable consideration with solid scores qualifying for lower rates on major loans.

HOW TO ADD POSITIVE ACCOUNTS TO A CREDIT REPORT

Start with a Secured Card

If this is your first time or you have had credit troubles before, a secured card requires a cash deposit as collateral but reports payments monthly. Use it wisely for small recurring charges like gas and pay the full balance so it shows on-time payments. After several months, ask if you can now have a regular card.

Check into Small Installment Loans

For building a mix of credit types reported, look at loans from credit unions for $1,000 or less since lending small amounts shows a willingness to borrow responsibly. Make your payments on the scheduled due date every month to improve your payment history.

See If Friends Will Add You

Ask trusted loved ones if you can be added as an authorized user to their existing credit card accounts. Reporting their long positive payment history will boost your scores faster than starting from scratch alone. Make sure not to abuse the card, or it could backfire.

Be Patient with Progress

Remember, credit scores take time to improve as positive behavior continues showing up on reports. Staying on top of on-time payments for secured credit cards, loans, and authorized user accounts over 6-12 months at least builds up your track record to more easily qualify for better financing offers in the future. Bit by bit, you'll see higher scores in less than a year.

HOW TO BUILD A STRONG CREDIT HISTORY

Building good credit is important. With a strong credit history, you'll have more options for loans, credit cards, and other financial products. It can also help you get a job or apartment! However, where do you start in building a good credit history? Here are tips to help you.

Open a Credit Card

One of the best ways to establish credit is by getting a credit card. Look for a basic card with no annual fees from a major bank or credit union. Only charge what you can easily pay off each month - try keeping your balances around 30% or less of your limit. Paying on time, every time, is key. This shows lenders you're responsible.

Make Payments on Time

Paying bills promptly is crucial. Set up automatic payments if you need to, but don't let anything go late. Even one missed or delayed payment can hurt your score. Your goal is to keep all accounts in "good standing."

Keep Credit Card Balances Low

It's best to charge a small portion of your credit limits each month. The percentage of available credit you're using is factored into your score. A high balance looks risky to lenders. Try not to go over 30% on one card.

Check Your Credit Report

Review your credit reports at AnnualCreditReport at least once a year. Errors can happen, so it's smart to check for inaccuracies. Dispute anything incorrect right away so your real history shows through. Knowing your reports could also help you watch for signs of fraud.

Sign Up for Credit Monitoring

Some credit monitoring services allow you to check your reports and scores more often. This can help catch identity theft or other issues early. While not 100% necessary, credit monitoring offers comfort and peace of mind for a small monthly or annual fee.

STRATEGIES FOR KEEPING YOUR CREDIT UTILIZATION LOW

One helpful strategy is paying down credit card balances before statement dates so reported amounts stay low compared to credit limits. You could also try making an extra payment mid-month. Aim to keep utilization under 30% of all available credit.

Check if issuers offer credit limit increases without applications so you can spread out spending across higher limits. This reduces the percentage used without changing spending habits.

Requesting occasional small credit limit raises when possible without hard pulls also benefits utilization. Be sure not to see increased ceilings as an excuse to over-spend beyond your means.

Set monthly spending caps well under credit lines as an extra buffer against slip-ups like unexpected bills. Also, stay in the practice of paying statements down every month to avoid costly interest charges.

Diversifying Your Mix

Having different types of credit accounts reporting shows lenders a well-established history. While diligently paying one starter credit card, small personal loans from banks or credit unions should also be considered, demonstrating the ability to repay various products.

In time, additionally having an auto loan, student loan, or mortgage report diversifies types further while strengthening the overall credit profile. Be sure adding new debt doesn't detract from keeping utilization rates low and maintaining positive payment records across all accounts.

Steady progress mixes your regularly reported credit types and lowers balances portioned across several accounts. This assures the highest possible scores when pursuing financing offers for bigger life goals in the future. Consistency is key long-term for maximum creditworthiness.

KEY TAKEAWAYS

- Good credit means you pay all bills on time.
- Start slow with cards where you fund the first and always pay back before due dates.
- Safe loans from credit unions are another way to prove you handle credit well.
- Letting others add you as an authorized user on their longtime accounts helps your credit history.

- Use less than 30% of your available credit and mix up card types when you can for higher scores.

It helps to use credit cards wisely. The next chapter provides tips on choosing the right card and making payments on time to improve your credit score.

7

SMART USE OF CREDIT CARDS

W hile improperly managing credit cards can damage your scores, when used judiciously, they can be a boon in building a positive credit history. This chapter discusses how to choose the right credit card for your needs. Different card types include secured options for rebuilding credit, low-interest cards to keep costs down, and rewards cards if you're confident you can avoid interest charges.

From there, sticking to good credit habits like always paying your statement balance each month, keeping balances below 30% of your limits, and never falling behind on payments can seriously strengthen your standing. The chapter will also cover common pitfalls, like not having a plan to pay off big spending, applying for too many new accounts in a short period, and only making the bare minimum payments without decreasing balances. With a bit of savvy, credit cards can become a trusted tool for establishing creditworthiness in less than a year.

HOW CREDIT CARDS CAN BE VALUABLE TOOLS FOR BUILDING CREDIT

Report Monthly Payments

One of the most important ways credit cards can help build your credit history is through reporting monthly payment activity to the major credit bureaus. Making at least the minimum payment due on time every single billing cycle shows lenders you are responsible and can manage credit responsibly. This consistent on-time payment history boosts your credit scores noticeably.

However, it's even better if you can manage to make payments higher than the minimum required each month. Large credit card balances carried month to month accruing high-interest fees will damage your credit utilization ratio reported. Paying the bare minimum also means debts linger longer. Aim to pay down account statements in full periodically, if possible, to avoid interest charges altogether.

Even if full payment isn't realistic currently due to other debt obligations, conscientiously paying a bit extra each cycle towards principal balances will start lowering what's owed quicker. Extra $20-50 applied to the highest interest rate card speeds payoff while also maintaining a positive credit history reported for years. The discipline of keeping accounts current and reducing reported spending builds solid credibility when larger loans are pursued.

Add Credit Mix Variety

Having different types of credit account reporting shows lenders a well-established credit profile developed through handling various credit products responsibly. While focused first on dutifully using one secured credit card or two, also aim to take on a small revolving credit union loan in the $500-$1000 range after several on-time payments, which displays financial management skills.

In a few years, when both that starter loan and credit cards continue reporting timely payments, adding a first auto loan financing a reliable vehicle builds another positive account type. Having personal loans, credit cards, and auto loans reported demonstrates proficiency with diverse credit instruments. Student loans, mortgages, business loans, and even credit limits on store cards contribute further to credit history.

Be certain adding installment loans or more revolving accounts doesn't detract from maintaining or paying down balances for current obligations first. The long-term goal remains to establish lengthy payment records exhibiting money mastery over an assortment of credit products without ever defaulting or handling debt carelessly. Variety strengthens while responsibility cements the greatest credit standing.

Start Building Credit Early

Kicking off credit building from a younger age by establishing starter credit card accounts or becoming authorized users on parents' mature accounts allows maximum time to benefit from favorable credit reporting. This influences your future scores. Consistency with responsible card usage solidifies creditworthiness much earlier in life than waiting until adulthood.

Adding a low-limit secured credit card requires a refundable security deposit as early as age 18 with parental approval. Charging small recurring costs helps report positive payment histories over many more years than waiting. Making on-schedule minimum payments for cell phone bills, gas, or subscription services develops reliability seen for decades ahead.

HOW TO CHOOSE THE RIGHT CREDIT CARD

Secured Cards

A secured card can be a wise first option if you don't have an extensive credit history. With these cards, you provide a cash deposit that becomes your credit limit. For example, if you deposit $200, your credit limit will be $200.

The deposit is typically held in a bank account by the card issuer. As long as you make all payments on time, you will get the deposit back after a period of responsible use, often within 6 to 12 months. Then, you may be eligible to upgrade to an unsecured card without a deposit requirement.

Using a secured card shows credit bureaus that you can manage credit responsibly, even with a small starting limit. Make small purchases each month and pay the full statement balance by the due date. This helps establish a positive on-time payment history over 6-12 months. If possible, look for no annual fee as well.

Low-Interest Cards

It's always best, if possible, to avoid interest charges by paying your full statement balance each month when using a credit card. However, sometimes, carrying a small balance for a month or two is unavoidable. If that's your situation, then a low-interest card is important.

Be sure to compare APRs across different cards. Aim for as low as possible, ideally under 15% interest if you can find it. The longer a balance stays unpaid, the more overall interest charges will add up at high rates.

Cutting the interest rate a couple of percentage points through a low-rate card will substantially lower your costs. Be sure to understand how long an introductory or promotional rate may last as well. After that initial timeframe, the regular higher rate will apply if the balance isn't paid off.

Rewards Cards

Credit cards that offer rewards programs give cardholders incentives to use the card through earning cashback, points, or airline miles with purchases. While these cards are great if you pay your full statement balance each month, be cautious of higher interest rates.

Look at your typical spending categories, such as groceries, gas, and dining out, and see what types of rewards different cards offer for these purchases. Choose a card that matches your top spending areas for maximum rewards accumulated. Pay attention to annual fees and premium cards.

Many card issuers allow you to cash in rewards for gift cards or merchandise or apply your earnings to your card balance as statement credits. Check the fine print to understand reward expiration policies and limits to earning or redemption. The responsible use of a rewards card that is aligned with your usual spending is a nice perk when building credit habits.

COMMON CREDIT CARD PITFALLS TO AVOID

Carrying High Balances

One of the easiest ways to hurt your credit scores is carrying large balances on your cards month after month. As mentioned earlier, if possible, keep balances below 30% of your credit limits. The higher your balances compared to limits, the greater the risk seen by lenders. Pay down balances to avoid this pitfall.

Applying for Multiple Cards at Once

While opening several new accounts may seem enticing for higher limits or different reward perks, it's always best to space out new credit applications. Each application results in a hard inquiry on your credit reports, which can temporarily lower scores by a small amount. Multiple inquiries in a short time frame signal risk to lenders.

Falling Into the Minimum Payment Trap

It may feel good to make the monthly minimum payments, but you'll end up paying more in interest charges if balances carry over. Minimum payments barely cover interest most times, so principal balances stay high. Try to pay as much over minimums as your budget allows you to pay off debt faster. Calculate payments needed to have an item paid off in 3 years to clear debt efficiently.

Missing or Late Payments

Nothing undoes positive credit building like missed, late, or underpayments. Set up automatic payments or calendar alerts to avoid slip-ups. Even one 30-day late mark or underpayment can stay on your record for years. Protect your reports by paying on time, in full, each month.

Closing Old Accounts

It's important to keep your oldest credit lines open to lengthen your credit history. Closing an old, no-annual-fee card you rarely use, though, is generally fine. Close cards if you've had them for 10+ years or if annual fees are not worth the age of history boost.

Hopefully, these tips will help you avoid common mistakes many make with credit cards. Remember, responsible use is key to maintaining excellent credit-worthiness.

HOW TO MANAGE MULTIPLE CREDIT CARDS

It's easy to accumulate several credit cards. With a wallet full of plastic, keeping track of payments and balances can get confusing. However, staying organized is important for maintaining good credit. Here are tips for managing multiple credit cards effectively:

Getting Started

The first step is taking inventory of all your cards. Take them out and lay them side by side on a table. Jot down key details for each: the issuer, the credit limit, the current balance, and the APR. This will help you assess which cards need more attention.

Next, make sure you have login credentials handy for paying and checking balances online. Many issuers offer website portals or apps for managing accounts digitally. Logging in regularly is important for oversight and timely payments. If you've lost track of login info, get in touch with issuers to get the details sorted.

Organizing Paperwork

With multiple cards comes multiple paper statements each month. Staying on top of payments requires keeping track of due dates. A good organizing system will save you late fees and aggravation.

Some people like putting each statement in a designated spot, like a labeled folder or drawer. Others opt to enter due dates on a calendar as soon as statements arrive. Pick whichever approach works best for your lifestyle and tendencies.

Designating Cards

Having a strategy for card usage can make reconciliation much simpler. For example, you might assign one card for food or gas and another for bills or utilities. You can mark cards with colored tape for quick visual identification.

Spending discipline also pays off. Limiting each card's transactions to a single category limits confusion when checking statements. Sticking to designated purposes means it's always obvious which statements tie to which receipts without digging.

Paying Bills on Time

Meeting minimum payment obligations is a bare minimum responsibility as a cardholder. However, constantly rolling over balances with interest is expensive. If you're able, aim to pay statements in full each month to avoid finance charges entirely.

That goal is easier to attain with methods that automate your payments. Sign up for autopay so funds are automatically transferred on due dates. You can set calendar reminders leading up to each due date so you remember to initiate payments manually in time.

Allocating Payments Effectively

When funds are tight, prioritizing card payments matters. Target the cards with the highest interest rates first to maximize interest savings. Paying minimums on all accounts except the card with the priciest APR is a savvy approach.

Keeping Track Online

Most issuers let you view all your card activity and balances in one location online after linking accounts. Taking advantage of these online dashboards streamlines oversight. At-a-glance statistics on total balances, available credit, and utilization ratios keep you informed on your overall credit picture monthly.

Re-Evaluating Offers

With each passing year, issuers may extend higher credit limits or improve terms on established accounts. These upgrades can present good chances to reorganize your card strategy.

If an older card gains a higher credit limit, consider shifting active balances over to take advantage of more breathing room. Freeing up a card also allows closing inactive accounts to declutter your wallet and credit report. Closures remove unavailable credit that influences credit utilization calculations, potentially boosting scores by a few points.

KEY TAKEAWAYS

- Cards help you build credit if used correctly and not swiped all the time.
- Pick cards that suit your spending, like one with rewards or a low-interest offer.
- You can only charge what you can pay back before the due date—not more than 30% of your limit.
- Avoid late fees by setting autopay or paying bills as soon as they arrive each month.
- Be smart, and don't open too many new cards too quickly. Also, pay off promotional balances before interest kicks in.

Loans are an important part of building credit strength. See what the next chapter has to say about choosing the right loans and making regular payments on time.

8

UNDERSTANDING AND MANAGING LOANS

This chapter discusses the role that different types of loans play in your financial life and credit reports. Taking the right loan at the right time can have benefits, but it must be handled properly. The chapter will go over loan types like personal loans, auto loans for buying a car, student loans, and mortgages. You'll learn what effect each loan type has on your score.

The book provides handy strategies like setting up autopay to make repayment simpler. You'll also learn about options for consolidating multiple smaller loans into one. Understanding the connection between loans and credit is important, too, when making long-term money moves. The chapter will wrap up by exploring how installment loans, in particular, can boost factors in your file and aid your fiscal planning.

HOW LOANS PLAY A SIGNIFICANT ROLE IN YOUR CREDIT PROFILE

Loans are an important part of managing your finances and building your credit history. Whether you need funds for an emergency, a large purchase, or to pay for education, loans provide access to capital when you need it most. However, it's important to understand how taking on debt through loans can affect your credit profile over both the short and long term. Here is how loans play a significant role in building or hampering your credit profile.

HOW LOAN ACCOUNTS AFFECT YOUR CREDIT SCORES

Whenever you take out a new loan, an inquiry is made against your credit reports. A hard inquiry occurs when a lender pulls your full credit history to evaluate your creditworthiness, and multiple inquiries in a short timeframe can negatively impact scores slightly. However, the impact is minor and temporary. What matters most is establishing a positive payment history to build credit.

Installment loan accounts, such as personal loans, auto loans, and mortgages, are reported on credit reports monthly after opening. On-time payments help demonstrate responsible debt management, which boosts credit scores. Late or missed payments damage scores significantly. Paying down balances also benefits scores by lowering credit utilization ratios.

Revolving credit accounts report balances but not specific payment history. Credit mix, or having both revolving and installment loan accounts open, can slightly benefit scores with responsible use. Closing long-standing accounts may lower the average age of accounts, which has a small negative effect.

Keeping Loans in Good Standing

The best way to ensure loans positively impact your credit long-term is by keeping all accounts in good standing through on-time payments. Here are tips:

- **Automate payments when possible.** Set up automated payments through your bank to ensure timely payments without the risk of missed or late ones.
- **Pad budget for extra expenses.** Add a cushion to monthly budgets to cover unexpected costs that could interfere with loan payments.
- **Communicate issues proactively.** If unexpected hardship arises, contact lenders right away to discuss options like short-term

leniency or modification to prevent damaging delinquencies.

- **Pay more than minimums when affordable.** Paying down balances faster through higher-than-minimum payments relieves ongoing interest costs and improves credit utilization.
- **Check reports yearly for errors.** Review credit reports at AnnualCreditReport.com to ensure lenders report payment history in a timely and accurate manner. Dispute errors immediately.
- **Keep balance-to-limit ratios low on revolving accounts.** Reduced credit utilization signals responsible use of available credit, which positively affects scores.

Building Credit without Loans

While loans play an important credit-building role, they aren't the only path. If you've started establishing credit or prefer avoiding debt, here are alternatives to consider:

- **Secured Credit Cards:** If you have a limited credit history, secured cards offer a low spending limit backed by a refundable cash deposit with the issuer. On-time payments are reported and can help expand credit selection.

- **Authorized User Cards:** Ask trusted family or friends with positive accounts if you can be added as an authorized user to benefit from their payment history reporting without individual responsibility for balances.
- **Retail Credit Cards:** Stores like department stores offer proprietary no-annual-fee cards with low credit lines reportable to bureaus. Responsible use builds payment records.
- **Loan Cosigning:** Serve as a cosigner to help others establish credit while reporting your on-time payments to bureaus. But understand you're responsible for balances if the primary borrower defaults.
- **Small Credit Builder Loans:** Some credit unions offer credit-builder loans with low monthly payments primarily structured to report positive payment history without access to funds for other use.

The Pathway to Strong Credit

Regardless of your starting point or preference for loans versus alternatives, establish reliable credit management habits. With growing responsible use of available credit options and keeping accounts current without late or missed payments reported, you pave the pathway to solid, reputable credit.

Your commitment now builds the foundation for accessing attractive rates on larger financial commitments like mortgages or auto loans in the future. With diligence, you can continually strengthen your credit profile through measured and viable steps gained each month spent building and demonstrating responsible financial habits.

TYPES OF LOANS AND HOW TO MANAGE THEM EFFECTIVELY

Now that you've learned the basics about how loans can affect your credit report, it's helpful to look more at common types of loans. Understanding the details of each will help you pick the best options for your needs and manage your payments correctly.

Personal Loans

Personal loans provide flexible funding, but how they affect your credit depends on how you make your payments. Since these are not secured by anything valuable, lenders will closely check your income, current debts, and credit scores to set the interest rate and payment terms.

- You can use the money for big purchases, combining debts, or personal costs without saying what it's for.
- Once approved, the money could be in your account within a few business days instead of waiting for credit card spending limits to go up.
- The full loan amount is given at once, and you agree to fixed monthly payments for the whole time, making budgets predictable.

However, consider how making payments on time affects your credit. To avoid harming your reports, it's smart to only borrow what you're sure you can repay based on a payment schedule. Set reminders in a calendar or autopay to help you avoid missing due dates by mistake. If you're struggling, work with lenders right away on options.

Auto Loans

Auto loans are commonly used to spread the total cost out in monthly payments. Lenders will look at your ability to pay back the auto loan by considering:

- **Payment history:** If you've paid other bills and used credit cards on time.
- **Income:** If you make enough money to cover the loan payments plus other monthly costs.

- **Down payment:** Bigger first payments mean smaller monthly payments and lower interest rates because you're financing a smaller remaining amount.

Making auto loan payments on time each month helps build your credit history. Make sure your steady income and budget allow on-time payments without too much financial stress. Refinancing for a lower interest rate may also cut long-term costs if your credit improves.

Student Loans

Student loans provide important options for continuing your education. Understanding the details of the loans helps make sure your payments fit with your future financial goals:

- Government loans often offer flexible payment plans based on income, help with interest costs, and forgiveness if you work in certain jobs.
- Private loans don't have the same benefits as government loans and charge variable interest rates based on your credit rather than rates in the economy.
- Government PLUS loans for parents and graduates also have variable rates, but getting

approved isn't guaranteed since they check
your credit.

To manage student loan balances responsibly, focus on
balancing school, work, and payments that fit within
your budget. Keeping track allows taking advantage of
lower rates and flexible payment options as the years
pass.

Mortgage Loans

As the largest debt most will undertake, it's critical to
get pre-approved for a home loan and understand
fully:

- **Down payment minimums:** At least 3-5% of
  the home's purchase price is typically required
  for conventional loans to avoid private
  mortgage insurance costs.
- **Credit scores and debt-to-income ratios:**
  Strong credit and low existing debt loads will
  qualify you for more affordable programs and
  rates.
- **Loan types:** Fixed-rate, adjustable-rate, FHA,
  VA, and USDA loans have different terms and
  requirements that are worth researching.
- **Closing costs:** Understand all fees associated
  with financing, inspections, and paperwork that

are due at closing in addition to your down payment amount.

With a mortgage, commit to keeping payments current at all times to protect homeownership status and investment. Holding the loan over decades is ideal for building invaluable credit longevity.

STRATEGIES FOR EFFECTIVE LOAN MANAGEMENT

Use Automatic Payments

Setting up automatic payments is a straightforward way to stay on top of payments. You authorize your bank to transfer funds from your checking or savings account to the lender on scheduled due dates. This keeps your accounts in good standing without the risk of late fees or missed payments. Be sure to have low balance alerts enabled in case funds get too low.

Consider Debt Consolidation

If you have multiple existing loans at different interest rates, consolidating them into one monthly payment at a lower consolidated rate could save money over the long run. Only do this to simplify paying off current obligations affordably, not to take on new debt.

Look into Refinancing

Once you've shown a responsible payment history and improved your credit rating, refinancing loans such as a mortgage, auto loan, or student loan may qualify you for better terms. Refinancing 1,000 at 0.5% lower interest over 5 years, for example, could save around 2,000 in total interest paid. However, be sure to factor in all closing fees to ensure projected net savings.

The goal is to use debt strategically while keeping on top of monthly dues. With careful planning, you can gradually strengthen your creditworthiness through the years.

THE RELATIONSHIP BETWEEN LOANS AND CREDIT

Many people need money for school, cars, or homes, so taking out loans is common. But did you know loans also impact your credit score? It's important to understand how loans connect to credit when borrowing money and keeping your score good.

What's in a Loan?

When you take a loan, you borrow a certain amount to pay it back. Your lender reports this debt to the major credit bureaus. Important details like the loan amount, your monthly payments, whether payments were made on time, and whether the loan is still open or closed become part of your credit history, affecting your credit score.

Consistently making on-time payments shows future lenders you are a safe borrower. However, late or missed payments can damage your score for years with a negative mark.

Importance of Credit Mix

Your credit reports and scores look at payment history and how you manage different types of credit, which is called your "credit mix." Reporting a loan proves you can responsibly handle an installment loan, along with things like credit cards, as part of your overall credit mix. A good mix signals different borrowing abilities.

How Long Does Payment History Matter?

Closed loans still influence your credit history. Past payment behaviors remain on reports for up to 10 years, showing later lenders your borrowing history. Even paid loans help future applications as creditors see your long credit report. Paying obligations through the end shows long-term trust.

Keeping loans in good standing means more access to affordable future credit and higher scores from all your hard work. Understanding the strong connection between loans and credit will help with all your borrowing needs.

HOW INSTALLMENT LOANS CAN POSITIVELY IMPACT YOUR CREDIT MIX

Taking the right types of installment loans can help you build strong credit. Some people think all loans arc bad for your finances, but that's not true. By understanding how creditors look at your credit reports, you can use certain loan products strategically to strengthen your credit mix.

What Is Credit Mix?

When companies review your credit reports to check whether you qualify for new credit cards, an auto loan, or a mortgage, they don't just look at your credit score. They also consider your "credit mix," which refers to the different types of accounts you have open and actively using. A good credit mix shows responsibility for managing different loan obligations successfully over many years.

A balanced credit mix includes a few open revolving credit accounts, such as credit cards and installment loans, reported on your reports monthly. Revolving accounts require minimum monthly payments but don't have set payoff dates. On the other hand, installment loans give you a fixed amount upfront that you agree to pay back through equal payments over a specific period.

While revolving credit, like credit cards, can lower your ratio as you use more available credit each month, the right installment loans don't have to impact that ratio at all if you pay on time. They strengthen other important credit factors. Here is how installment loans can help in building your credit profile healthily.

THE BENEFITS OF INSTALLMENT LOANS

Installment loans reporting to the major credit bureaus demonstrate you can assume larger debt responsibly and manage payments consistently over the years. This establishes what's called your "credit tenure" - the length of time you've actively used different credit lines. A longer credit history with diverse accounts shows lenders you know how to take on debt and handle repayment.

- **Payment history**—Each on-time installment loan payment builds your record of punctuality. This heavy-weighted factor reports your payment performance on all accounts.

- **Credit mix** - A diverse mix of revolving and installment accounts establishes you can manage different credit obligations responsibly over the years. This variety raises your creditworthiness in the eyes of future lenders.
- **Credit utilization** - Installment loans don't impact your credit utilization ratio since the amount owed isn't reported monthly like revolving accounts. This preserves your available credit usage.
- **Credit age** - New installment loans help increase your average age of accounts over the long run by starting new credit lines reporting for 7-10 years. This builds your credit tenure gradually.

By adding the right installment loans to your credit mix judiciously over the years, you can see a slow but steady strengthening in your debt management reputation across these critical factors.

MANAGING MULTIPLE INSTALLMENT ACCOUNTS WISELY

While diverse debt demonstrates creditworthiness, too many open loans increase minimum payments that could overwhelm your budget. Therefore, spacing out new installment accounts is key as you strengthen your credit steadily over the years.

- Focus on autopay enrollment to prevent late fees from hectic schedules interfering with due dates.
- Check monthly statements closely for payment amounts changing seasonally or annually as agreed initially.
- In case of unexpected periods without income, maintain an emergency savings balance larger than the total minimum monthly installment payments.
- Consider consolidating older installment loans together if interest rates are substantially lower on a new combined loan. But pay off ballooning balances first to avoid owing more.
- Continually monitor for refinancing opportunities, lowering the interest cost of performing installment loans through better credit scores.

By using installment accounts judiciously as credit-building tools through diligent payments, your debt management reputation grows demonstrably stronger with each line of credit initiated. Remember, the tried-and-true path of slow, steady effort yields long-lasting credit strength for future large purchases on healthier borrowing terms.

KEY TAKEAWAYS

- Loans like for cars or college show lenders you pay back bigger debts.
- Different loans affect your credit in different ways - auto helps longer than credit cards.
- Set up automatic payments so you never miss a due date by mistake.
- Refinance when rates go down to keep payments cheaper and credit looking good.
- Consolidate small loans into bigger ones to simplify payments.

There are handy methods beyond regular accounts for strengthening your credit foundation. Turn to the next chapter to discover add-on options like authorized user status and rent reporting that add positively to your credit score.

9

LEVERAGING CREDIT BUILDING TOOLS

While paying down debt and watching credit usage takes time, there are additional strategies that can give your credit-building efforts an immediate boost. In this chapter, you'll learn about valuable tools like secured credit cards, credit builder loans, and becoming an authorized user on a trusted family or friend's established credit card account.

Did you know rent and utility payments can also be reported? Bringing positive payment histories into your credit file lends reliability. The chapter will look at how leveraging different reporting methods provides a significant advantage if you want a head start on credit success. If you're rebuilding credit more holistically, alternative data like your telecom and subscription services payment history can contribute to your score. Taking full advantage of available options helps your credit profile become balanced and demonstrates your responsible handling of financial obligations.

TOOLS TO HELP BUILD AND IMPROVE YOUR CREDIT SCORES

Building good credit is an important part of managing your finances well. While it may seem daunting, there are user-friendly tools that can help you establish credit or boost scores if they need improvement. Here are the top options:

Secured Credit Cards

One great path is a secured credit card. With this type of card, you put down a refundable security deposit, about 200-300, and that amount becomes your credit limit. The card reports your payments to the major credit bureaus like a regular credit card. This lets you demonstrate responsible credit habits while protecting the issuer in case of missed payments.

As you use the card for smaller monthly expenses and pay the statement balance in full each month, lenders will see you handling credit wisely. After six months to a year of on-time payments, many card issuers will convert secured cards to regular, unsecured cards with higher limits as trust is built. Be aware that typical interest rates are high with these starter cards since the risk is greater. However, the credit building makes them worth considering if scores need a boost.

Credit Builder Loans

Credit builder loans work by reporting loan installments to the credit bureaus. With these programs, you borrow a small amount—say $300—and make fixed monthly repayments for 6-12 months. The money isn't really for spending; it sits in an account collecting interest as you pay it back. Completing the cycle adds positive information to your credit files. Look for rotating payment options that report balances to ensure full utilization benefits.

A bonus of credit builder loans is that you get the deposited funds back once the loan is fulfilled. Be sure origination or maintenance fees don't outweigh the credit gains. Programs through credit counseling agencies or community banks tend to have the best terms. Like with secured cards, the goal is to demonstrate timely payments over many statement periods.

Becoming an Authorized User

If your credit needs work but you don't qualify for the previous options yet, you have the option of becoming an authorized user. This involves piggybacking on the good credit of someone you trust, like a family member, who adds you as a user to one of their long-standing credit cards or loans. Their good payment history will then merge with yours on credit reports.

While it may seem like a shortcut, authorized user status has helped many correct past credit mistakes or thin files. Be certain your sponsor truly understands the responsibility involved. Select someone committed to keeping balances low and payments current. Also, understand that you have no legal obligation for the debt, but it will impact both credit profiles positively and negatively going forward.

HOW RENT AND UTILITY PAYMENTS CAN BOOST YOUR CREDIT SCORE

Paying your rent and utility bills on time each month is important for having a place to live. But did you know these payments can help improve your credit score? Your rental history and how you pay your energy bills may boost your credit score in the long run. A higher credit score means you'll qualify for loans and credit cards later on with better interest rates.

Renting Makes Up Credit History

When you rent an apartment or house, the landlord or property manager has the option to report your rent payments to the major credit bureaus, similar to other lines of credit. Not all landlords do this yet, but more are realizing tenants can benefit too. Having rent reported helps build your credit file if you don't have a credit card or loan history yet. It also fills in gaps in your credit history if you haven't had an open account for a while.

Credit reports allow future lenders to see how reliably you pay monthly bills. Showing rent has been paid on time each month shows potential creditors that you handle payments consistently. The reduced risk means you could get better terms later when financing is needed. Keep making all payments as agreed, and your credit score will gradually increase as positive rent payments are reported each month.

Keep Utility Bills Current

Many utility companies have programs where they report your payment history and activity directly to the credit bureaus. Keeping current with all of these regular bills demonstrates responsibility with monthly obligations, which credit scores consider. Set up automatic payments if possible so bills are always paid on time, and you avoid late fees by accident.

Look into the payment reporting programs your landlord and utility providers offer to sign up. They allow the sharing of positive payment data, which benefits your credit over 12-24 months of on-time payments. Not all companies participate, though, so check carefully if the option exists for where you live and get services. Signing up requires paperwork but has worthwhile benefits.

Build a Strong Rental History

It typically takes 6-12 months of consistent, on-time monthly reports before you start seeing an improvement in your credit score. So, keep payments up without exception to get the full positive impact over the longer term. You could see your credit score increase by 20-50 points or more after a full year or two of every payment reported on schedule.

Rental and utility payment information helps round out your credit history and score if credit applications are limited. It provides another way to demonstrate responsible financial handling of regular monthly bills beyond credit cards. The reporting turns things you were already paying monthly into a credit account. Consider checking into available programs if boosting your credit is an important goal.

ALTERNATIVE CREDIT DATA

As you work to establish credit or improve credit scores, it's good to know about alternative data that can supplement traditional credit accounts. Alternative data refers to your payment history on nontraditional lines like utilities, telecom services, streaming subscriptions, and more. More sources reporting responsible use allow a fuller picture of how you manage financial obligations in everyday life.

Utility and Telecom Payments

On-time bill payments to your mobile carrier, internet provider, or municipal utilities can help improve your credit. Many utility companies voluntarily contribute payment information to credit bureaus. When done over at least 6 months, the activity adds to credit files like revolving accounts or loans.

Check whether your providers participate in alternative data programs. They allow lending industry access with consumer consent under privacy rules. A few extra positives like these on reports reinforce you tackle bills responsibly, benefiting scores noticeably. It creates credit without always needing credit to establish credit, if that makes sense. Remember, payments reflect negatively.

Streaming Subscriptions

Millions rely on digital subscriptions for music, videos, news, cloud services, and more nowadays as alternatives to cable. While you likely aren't building credit directly with these, payment performance still underwrites your financial credibility. Certain membership platforms share on-time status with credit bureaus when opted-in.

Consider linking subscriptions to checking accounts, debit and credit cards, or digital wallets for autopay. Not only does it ensure subscription renewal without late fees, but consistent subscription tracking also builds profiles as if these were regular monthly revolving accounts. Credit bureaus can factor subscription data into algorithms assessing risk levels like traditional lines of credit.

Employment and Income Verification

While credit reports measure liability management through debt, underwriting also examines the ability to repay through present and future earning power. Alternative data validation services verify applicant employment, income amount, and work history directly with companies for a more robust risk picture that combines traditional credit factors plus additional soft variables.

When completing applications, see if eligibility checks consider outside earnings services. They pull securely from employer databases - not traditional credit files - to substantiate income evidence without always needing lengthy tax transcripts or pay stubs up front as sole proof.

KEY TAKEAWAYS

- Secured credit cards require a deposit, but treat them like regular cards to build your score.
- Small signature loans let you establish paying back money monthly.
- Becoming an authorized user on a family member's longtime account mixes in their good history.
- Rental payments can demonstrate responsibility, too, if your housing reports payments to credit bureaus.
- Alternative data like phone and utility bills can help those thin on traditional credit by showing you pay what you owe.

Hard work only pays off if you keep up healthy credit habits. Turn to the last chapter for ongoing maintenance tips to guard your credit score.

10

MAINTAINING GOOD CREDIT FOR THE LONG-TERM

I n this last chapter, you'll learn that getting a good score is half the battle. Keeping it top-notch is also important. The chapter will cover why it's crucial to regularly check your reports and make sure nothing looks off. There are habits to avoid, like missing payments or maxing out most of your credit limits, that can bring your score down if you're not careful.

Preparing yourself for major purchases or unexpected costs with a safety cushion is key, too. This chapter will also look at staying informed, as reporting practices change often. Most importantly, being proactive to protect your hard work over the long haul is key. Your score impacts many financial opportunities, so staying vigilant unlocks rewards like lower loan rates and increased flexibility. Maintaining excellent credit is worth the effort for years of savings.

THE IMPORTANCE OF REGULARLY MONITORING AND MAINTAINING CREDIT

Your credit score plays a big role in many aspects of your financial life. From getting loans and credit cards to renting an apartment, that three-digit number can open or close many doors for you. That's why it's so important not to focus on building good credit but on maintaining it, too.

Checking In Regularly

One of the best things you can do is check your credit reports at least once a year. Errors happen, and you should catch them before they cause problems down the line. All three major credit bureaus - Equifax, Experian, and TransUnion - allow you to get a free copy of your credit report once every 12 months from AnnualCreditReport. Spread these out so you're checking in with one bureau every 4 months.

Review your reports thoroughly, making sure all the information listed is accurate. Pay close attention to personal details like your name, address, Social Security number, and employment. Also, check for accounts or loans you didn't open yourself. Signs of identity theft could be lurking. If you spot errors or suspicious activity, contact the credit bureau and work to get it corrected or removed right away.

Keeping Accounts Active

It's not enough to pay your bills on time - you need to keep using credit moderately to maintain your score. Lenders want to see that you can responsibly manage different types of credit products.

If you have credit cards, make small purchases monthly and pay the full statement balance by the due date. This shows responsible use without racking up debt. For loans or lines of credit like an auto loan or home equity line, maintain a low balance relative to the total available credit. Closed or inactive accounts drag your score down, so speak to card issuers before closing old accounts if you don't need them anymore.

Addressing Issues Early

If you miss a payment due to forgetfulness or a financial hiccup, don't panic. Contact the lender right away to check if you can work out a one-time waiver. Be ready to get current again promptly to reverse the damage.

Collection accounts and bankruptcies stay on your reports for years, so seek credit counseling if you're unable to keep up with serious financial struggles. With time and following advice, counselors can help you work out a solution to eventually bounce back. The key is addressing issues early before they mushroom.

BEHAVIORS THAT CAN DAMAGE CREDIT AND HOW TO AVOID THEM

Keeping good credit is an important part of managing your finances well. With discipline and smart practices, your credit can grow stronger. However, certain behaviors should be avoided, as they can negatively impact your credit scores. Here are the habits to steer clear of and protect your credit.

Avoiding Late and Missed Payments

One of the best things you can do is always pay bills on time. Even missing a single payment by 30 days can seriously damage your credit. Set up autopay or calendars so due dates don't slip your mind. If you're ever struggling, contact creditors right away - they'd rather work out a payment plan than report delinquency if possible. Late marks stay on records for 7 years and lower scores significantly, so do what it takes to avoid them.

Using Credit Responsibly

It's tempting to max out available credit when money feels tight, but too much owed versus limits damages scores. Ideal revolving account utilization is under 30% of limits. Pay balances steadily without going over the limit so creditors see disciplined credit control with rarely owing significant balances month to month. This demonstrates reliable repayment abilities to lenders.

Pacing Credit Applications

Each application produces a hard inquiry, denting scores slightly, but multiple requests in a short period suggest financial instability to lenders. Space out applications at least 6 months apart so scores aren't unnecessarily dragged down. Only apply for accounts you really need and can pay off timely. Too many recently opened lines also lower scores by diluting average account age.

Managing Derogatory Marks Properly

Records of bankruptcies, foreclosures, settlements, judgments, or liens stay on profiles for 7-10 years, penalizing scores greatly during that time. Once penalties expire, though, improve money habits and demonstrate rehabilitation as mentioned above to regain top-tier status. Lenders see you've learned from past issues.

HOW TO PREPARE FOR FUTURE FINANCIAL GOALS

It's smart to get ready for big expenses that may come up. Building good credit is a great start. Here are tips to help make your dreams a reality.

Save for Emergencies

Life doesn't always go as planned. Putting away even a little each month means you'll be okay if unexpected bills arrive or your job changes. Aim to save enough to cover 3 to 6 months of necessities like rent and food. That way, upcoming goals feel within reach no matter what happens.

Save for Major Costs

Things like college, a house, a new car, retirement, or a wedding are expensive. You need to start saving years before to make it work. Figure out estimated costs and break them into small monthly amounts to contribute from each paycheck. Researching gives you a plan to pay for things affordably. Strong credit opens options when savings fall short, so take good care of it.

Stay on Top of Credit Changes

Rules and lending change. Keep learning new ways to handle your finances safely. Check for updates from the bureaus on your rights. Subscribe to sources that can maximize your options. Knowledge is power when qualifying for important loans.

Together, good credit habits, emergency savings, and smart long-term planning using today's best strategies mean big life plans feel within reach, thanks to preparing wisely now. Careful saving over the years pays off with happy returns.

THE IMPORTANCE OF CONSISTENTLY MAINTAINING A HEALTHY CREDIT SCORE

Now that you know how important it is to keep an eye on your credit, it'll help you learn how to maintain a healthy score. Like your physical health, your credit score needs regular care and monitoring to stay in good shape. Like how healthy habits help you feel better every day, good credit habits can benefit your finances in many ways, including:

Lower Interest Rates and More Savings

One of the best perks of a stellar credit score is saving money through lower interest rates. Lenders see a high score as low risk. They know you've proven yourself as a responsible borrower, so they'll reward you with better rates on loans, credit cards, and more. A difference of 1% can put hundreds or thousands back in your pocket when repaying debt. Every point your score increases puts extra cash in your wallet.

More Flexibility with Borrowing

In addition to interest, your creditworthiness impacts other terms like loan amounts, repayment periods, and fees. Solid credit opens the door to more flexible financing options when you need them most, like a larger home or auto loan. It also means the ability to borrow in a pinch, whether it's a personal loan to consolidate debt or a credit card with a higher limit for emergencies. Maintaining excellent credit ensures you have access when opportunities arise.

Peace of Mind

Tending to your credit score provides financial security and removes stress. Instead of worrying about applications or wondering "What if?" you can confidently know you're approved for new accounts. Problems are less likely to arise with vigilant credit maintenance, too. So enjoy the freedom that comes with keeping credit in tip-top shape through continuous learning and healthy habits.

Rental and Insurance Savings

Landlords check credit before approving apartment applications. Solid credit means broader housing choices at competitive rates. It could save you from paying a higher security deposit. Insurance companies also use credit-based risk assessments. A high score may lower your premiums for auto, home, and other policies.

Employment Opportunities

An increasing number of employers review credit as part of background checks, especially for management roles. A pristine credit history demonstrates responsible decision-making and financial stability that hiring managers value. This gives you a competitive edge over other job applicants. Stellar credit opens occupational doors by signaling trustworthiness to potential employers.

KEY TAKEAWAYS

- Getting your credit score in good shape is only the beginning. You have to keep it that way.
- Check your report at least once a year so you can fix mistakes before things go wrong.
- Avoid late payments, maxing out credit cards, or opening many new accounts at the same time.
- Setting aside rainy-day savings and planning

big purchases will help you keep up with all payments.

- Taking care of your credit means better deals like low rates and more flexible financing options down the road. It pays to make it a long-term habit.

CONCLUSION

You've made it to the end of this book. Hopefully, you found the information helpful for understanding how to build and maintain your credit score in less than a year. When you started, credit reports weren't the easiest thing to grasp. However, going through real examples chapter by chapter likely helped make sense of it all.

By now, the basics of credit scores are clear - what the numbers mean, what impacts them, and how credit fits into many aspects of life. The book walked you through getting your reports to see where you stand. Did you spot mistakes? It also showed you how to dispute errors the right way.

You learned to create an effective credit score repair plan with goals, budgeting, and smart debt strategies. As the efforts gained steam, you got tips on adding positive accounts and using credit cards responsibly. The book outlined wise credit management when it comes to loans. Don't forget about extra credit-building resources, either.

So, how will you apply what you learned? Regardless of your situation, the techniques, exercises, and suggestions in this book offer solutions to fit your needs. You've now learned how to work on credit long-term by staying consistent and focused.

Remember, progress takes patience. Don't get discouraged if something doesn't immediately work out. Small wins are worth celebrating, too, like negotiating down a bill. Tracking achievements, both big and small, encourages during tough times.

As you nurture healthy credit habits, keep an eye on your situation. Regularly check credit reports and consider credit for major life decisions. Staying informed protects what you've worked hard to build. With a commitment to learning and smart credit practices, you can attain a good credit score in less than a year!

THANK YOU

I would like to thank all of the readers of my book for spending a few hours with me learning about a topic I am passionate about. I hope you were able to take away some key points that will help guide you to achieve the credit score you deserve. I wish you the best on your credit-building journey!

It would mean a lot if you could post a review. Reviews and feedback help give me the ability to continue writing books and sharing more valuable financial information with readers.

Go to this link: https://amzn.to/4cATQ2t or
Scan the QR code below:

REFERENCES

12 Good Reasons to Repair Your Credit. (n.d.). Www.linkedin.com. https://www.linkedin.com/pulse/ 12-good-reasons-repair-your-credit-debt-com

Cahill, J. (2024, May 30). The Importance of Credit Repair and Financial Education. Www.linkedin.com. https://www.linkedin.com/pulse/importance-credit-repair-financial-education-joshua-cahill-sfz2c/

Daly, L. (2020, April 8). How to Understand Your Credit Score: The Complete Guide | The Ascent. The Motley Fool. https://www.fool.com/the-ascent/credit-score-guide/

Dieker, N. (2022, December 20). How to Build Credit. Bankrate. https://www.bankrate.com/personal-finance/credit/how-to-build-credit/

How do I dispute an error on my credit report? (n.d.). Consumer Financial Protection Bureau. https://www.consumerfinance.gov/ask-cfpb/how-do-i-dispute-an-error-on-my-credit-report-en-314/

How do I get a free copy of my credit reports? (2023, August 28). Consumer Financial Protection Bureau. https://www.consumerfinance.gov/ask-cfpb/how-do-i-get-a-free-copy-of-my-credit-reports-en-5/

How Personal Loans Can Impact Your Credit Score -. (2024, April 30). IndusInd Bank. https://www.indusind.com/iblogs/categories/manage-your-finance/how-personal-loans-can-impact-your-credit-score/

How to Get Your Annual Credit Report from Experian - Experian. (n.d.). Www.experian.com. https://www.experian.com/help/annual-credit-report.html

Luthi, B. (2016, April 21). Understanding Credit Scores - Experian. Www.experian.com. https://www.experian.com/blogs/ask-experian/credit-education/score-basics/understanding-credit-scores/

Understand, get, and Improve Your Credit Score | USAGov. (2023, November 7). Www.usa.gov. https://www.usa.gov/credit-score

Understanding Credit. (n.d.). Financial Aid & Scholarships. https://financialaid.berkeley.edu/financial-liter acy-and-resources/understanding-credit/

What is a credit score and how does it work? (n.d.). Www.lloydsbank.com. https://www.lloydsbank.com/ understanding-credit/what-is-a-credit-score-how-does-a-credit-score-work.html

What is an Excellent Credit Score? | Equifax. (n.d.). Www.equifax.com. https://www.equifax.com/ personal/education/credit/score/articles/-/learn/ what-is-a-credit-score/

White, M. D. G. (2020, October 22). The beginner's guide to credit scores: How to understand and improve your credit score. CNBC. https://www.cnbc.com/ select/guide/credit-scores-for-beginners/

Made in the USA
Columbia, SC
06 September 2024

41906743R00095